THE SKILLFUL FORAGER

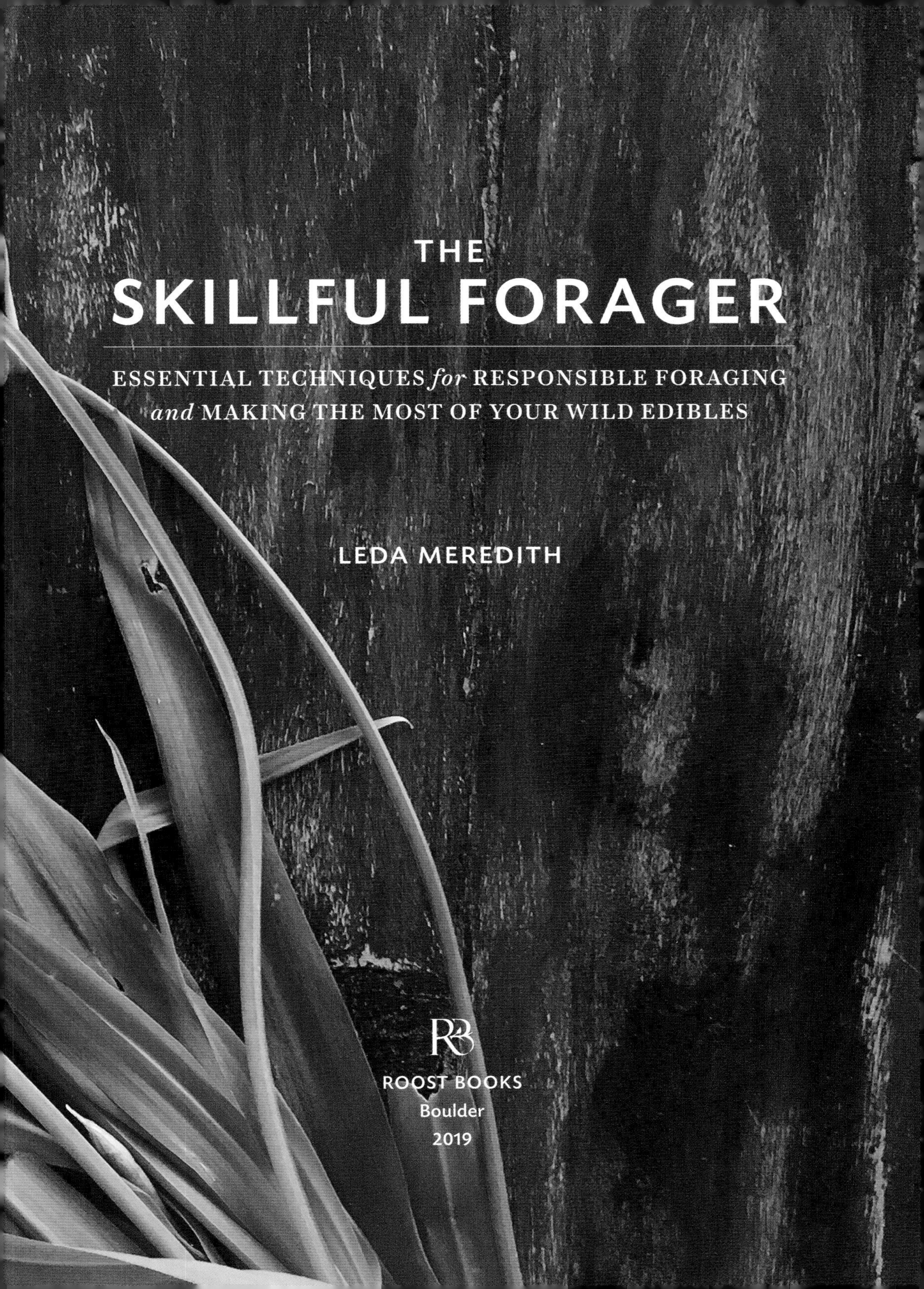

THE
SKILLFUL FORAGER

ESSENTIAL TECHNIQUES *for* RESPONSIBLE FORAGING
and MAKING THE MOST OF YOUR WILD EDIBLES

LEDA MEREDITH

R℔

ROOST BOOKS

Boulder

2019

Roost Books
An imprint of Shambhala Publications, Inc.
2129 13th Street
Boulder, Colorado 80302
roostbooks.com

Photography credits: Mike Krebill, pages 112, 140. Roey Orbach, pages 19, 88. Samuel Thayer, page 207. Jeremy Umansky, pages 83, 225, 230. Ellen Zachos, www.backyardforager.com, pages 118, 128, 130, 161, 175, 223. "Spore Print of the Week" by AJC1 from www.flickr.com/photos/47353092@N00/37475625491, page 226. All other photos are by the author.

Eating wild plants is very risky due to the nature of look-alike poisonous plants. The information presented here is thorough and accurate to the best of our knowledge, but it is essential that you always practice extreme caution and use your best judgment when foraging. Shambhala Publications and the author disclaim any and all liability in connection to the collection and consumption of wild plants and the use of the instructions in this book.

9 8 7 6 5 4 3 2

Printed in China

♾ This edition is printed on acid-free paper that meets the
American National Standards Institute Z39.48 Standard.
♻ Shambhala Publications makes every effort to print on recycled paper.
For more information please visit www.shambhala.com.

Roost Books is distributed worldwide by Penguin Random House, Inc., and its subsidiaries.

Designed by Laura Shaw Design

Library of Congress Cataloging-in-Publication Data
Names: Meredith, Leda, author.
Title: The skillful forager: essential techniques for responsible foraging and
making the most of your wild edibles / Leda Meredith.
Description: First edition. | Boulder: Shambhala, 2019. | Includes
bibliographical references and index.
Identifiers: LCCN 2018010052 | ISBN 9781611804836 (paperback: alk. paper)
Subjects: LCSH: Wild plants, Edible—Identification. | Cooking (Wild foods) |
Wild plants, Edible—Preservation.
Classification: LCC QK98.5.A1 M47 2019 | DDC 581.6/32—dc23
LC record available at https://lccn.loc.gov/2018010052

This book is dedicated to all the foragers who are going to disagree with me about what is the best method for working with this or that wild edible, claim ownership of a technique I describe (even if multiple others claim the same), or who are sure (and they may be right) that they have discovered a better way to work with a certain wild food.

Hello, dear ones. Long may this conversation continue.

CONTENTS

INTRODUCTION

A Twenty-First-Century Forager

I STARTED FORAGING IN THE 1960s. When I was around three years old, my great-grandmother took me to San Francisco's Golden Gate Park where she taught me how to identify a dandelion plant. We brought home a bagful of leaf rosettes (the leaves all connected with a thin sliver of root) and she showed me how to cook them up Greek-style. My great-grandmother had grown up on a small island in Greece where foraging (a word I'm sure she never knew) was normal.

Because her otherwise stern eyes twinkled with delight when we foraged for *horta* (the Greek word for wild edible greens of any kind), I was naturally curious. I wanted in on the joy that this plant brought to my *yia-yia*.

Foraging know-how had skipped a couple of generations in my family. My grandmother had learned from my great-grandmother, just as I was doing. But she didn't put the knowledge to use. In fact, she ran from it. She was a classic mid-twentieth-century wife welcoming newfangled appliances and frozen foods that promised to free her from the kitchen. She didn't think it was important to teach my mom about eating dandelions.

Long after my great-grandmother had passed away, I kept learning about and eating wild edibles. I still consider botanical field guides great reading. And when my first career as a professional dancer was coming to an end in my late thirties and early forties, and I needed to choose a next career, the first

A variety of wild edible fruits, mushrooms, flowers, and leaves harvested on a single summer afternoon.

thing that came to mind was wild plants. I had been passionate about plants as a hobby since those days in the park with great-grandma. Why not pursue that interest more intensely?

But not just any wild plants. I was mostly interested in the ones I could eat or use as medicine. And that interest in wild edible plants led to wild edible mushrooms and on and on. By my early fifties, I had already written one wild edible plants field guide as well as a wild foods cookbook. Why did I need to write a third book about foraging?

I needed to write this book because I wanted to teach a new generation of readers age-old foraging techniques as well as new ones. I need to share the knowledge that I got from my great-grandma and from my own years of experience. I need to share what my hands know as they feel their way up a wild asparagus shoot searching for the snapping point. I want you to know, too, how to tell the difference between the glossy, translucent basswood leaves that are delicious, and the already dull, matte leaves that will be unpleasantly tough.

When I wrote my third book—a field guide to wild edible plants in the Northeast—my publisher and I decided to leave out recipes so that we could include more plants: there wasn't room for both. When I wrote my wild foods cookbook, I had to limit it to just fifty plants because otherwise I wouldn't have been able to include all the recipes I wanted to share. And in neither was there space for the nitty-gritty of technique, including important knowledge such as the best time to dig up the root of a biennial like burdock or how to harvest the edible (and surprisingly tasty) part of bark without harming the tree.

The old-time wild edible food guides I read avidly in my youth sometimes gave recipes, but too often they contained dubious plant identification information. For example, they'd list a plant as pigweed but fail to give the scientific name (several plants share the common name "pigweed"). Or they combined accurate but densely technical botanical identifications with curt advice such as, "Roots good. Immature flower stalks also edible." Okay, but how do I turn that advice into dinner?

There is an enormous difference between "edible" and "good." Often that difference is less about which wild edible species you are gathering than the timing of your harvest or your preparation method. Knowing when to forage is just as important as knowing what to forage. In addition to which wild edible to select, which part of it to use, and when to harvest it, you need to know how to prepare it. With some wild edibles that is not a question of gustatory satisfaction but of safety.

As twenty-first-century foragers, we need to go beyond relearning what previous generations knew. We now have to deal with issues of pollution, legality, and sustainability that were not on my great-grandma's radar. The first two I discuss in part one; sustainable harvesting methods are a focus throughout the whole book.

With a big tip of the hat to other contemporary foraging authors who also go beyond field identification skills to share practical and sustainable foraging techniques, this book is my contribution to the ongoing work of reskilling people. By "reskilling," I mean teaching twenty-first-century foragers what my great-grandma (and maybe yours) already knew.

Whether you are just beginning your adventures with foraged food or are already an experienced gatherer, I am excited to share these skills with you. If I ever have the chance to pull up a chair at your table someday, I trust you'll be serving something wonderfully wild.

PART ONE

Getting Started

1

HOW TO USE
THIS BOOK

IF YOU ARE AN EXPERIENCED FORAGER, you might be tempted to skip straight to a wild edible ingredient that you know is currently in season and read up on my recommendations for harvesting, preparing, and preserving that particular type of wild food. That's fine: you may find tips that will improve your existing foraging skills. But first, take a moment to review the important foraging guidelines in chapter 2. These guidelines are the difference between damaging the landscape and being a forager whose efforts result in the win-win situation of delicious, healthy food *and* a thriving, sustainable ecosystem.

If you are new to foraging, be sure to read through all of part one, which includes the foraging guidelines, information about worthwhile gear, and a guide to when each type of wild ingredient is in season and in which type of location. This will spare you from looking for berries in a forest in April (there aren't any) or other frustrating wastes of your time. Once you have a better idea of what to look for at a certain time of year in a particular kind of location, look at the appropriate wild ingredient sections. First pay attention to the best harvesting practices: you can always reopen the book and look up preparation and preservation methods when you get home.

The harvesting methods detailed for each wild food type are not only sustainable but will enable you to collect the particular wild edible efficiently and at its most delicious stage. You'll also find "example plant" (or mushroom or seaweed) profiles for each category of wild food. The example plants are typical of that type of wild ingredient or especially widespread and easy for readers to find. For example, for plants that have edible leaves that grow in a rosette pattern *and* have edible roots, you'll find the dandelion. You'll learn where to find and how to identify the individual example plants but the instructions on how to harvest, prepare, and preserve apply to other wild edibles in that category as well. The book also includes profiles of wild edibles that I call "rule breakers." These are plants that need to be handled differently than others in their category. For example, although the fruits of the ginkgo tree are commonly referred to as "nuts," they are not actually nuts, and they do need to be cooked in order to render them edible.

The glossary clarifies botanical terms that new foragers may find unfamiliar. While I have tried as much as possible to keep the descriptions clear and non-technical, sometimes it has been necessary to use phrases such as "leaves that grow in a rosette."

You will also find a resources section with books, websites, and sources for tools mentioned in the book. Follow these recommendations at your own risk: foraging is addictive and so is the never-ending path of learning more about wild edibles.

2

THE NUTS AND BOLTS
OF FORAGING

THESE ARE THE ESSENTIALS that you need to know before a single berry goes into your mouth or you pull out your shovel to dig up some edible roots.

THE IMPORTANT STUFF

1. Always be 100 percent certain of your identification.
2. Gather with exuberant gratitude rather than greed.
3. Harvest only what you can use.
4. Use everything that you harvest.
5. If the wild edible you're looking at is endangered in that location, or scarce, leave it alone (no matter how delicious it is); or harvest using a method you are 100 percent certain will leave that species able to regrow.

HOW TO SAFELY GATHER WILD FOODS

What about Pollution?

Pollutants such as heavy metals and pesticides can contaminate wild plants through the soil or from the air. Places to be suspicious of toxic pollutants include near heavily trafficked roads, industrial agriculture farms, and your suburban neighbor's immaculate front yard (tons of chemicals are dumped on private property to ensure those perfectly verdant lawns). Also, be sure to check if there are any city- or area-wide pesticide spraying programs (as is the case in my hometown of New York City).

Harvesting in Suburbia

Aside from a patch of land that's directly downhill from an industrial farm, suburbia is the most dangerous landscape for foraging. Homeowners throw huge quantities of chemicals at their lawns and gardens to maintain that perfectly lush-yet-groomed look.

Ironically, that approach doesn't really work. Even after being blasted with chemicals, dandelions will reappear in the lawn, *Aegopodium* (goutweed) will emerge in the shaded borders, and Japanese knotweed will shoot up soon after being drenched with herbicides (albeit with weirdly wrinkled and discolored leaves).

In suburban landscapes, *always* be suspicious of toxic chemicals. Honestly, I usually just skip the suburbs altogether when foraging. You should always assume that golf courses and their surrounding grounds are loaded with chemicals too.

Harvesting Near Busy Streets and Highways

The usual rule of thumb is to harvest at least 50 feet away from a busy roadway. However, the reality is that the safe foraging distance is much more variable than that depending on whether you're downhill, uphill, or level with that road.

Remember that heavy metals are literally heavy. Because of this, if I am downhill from a heavily trafficked road, I do not harvest there unless I am considerably farther away from the road than the usual advice (I'd say as far as 100 feet). If I am level with the road, I'll go with the usual 50 feet rule. If I'm uphill from the road, I'll risk gathering considerably closer than that.

Wood sorrel (*Oxalis stricta*, *O. pes-caprae*, and other oxalis species) is a common weed in parks and gardens with a refreshing lemony flavor.

But on quiet, infrequently trafficked lanes, I've been known to gather mulberries and other fruit from street trees in cities (I would not, however, gather roots, shoots, or leaves growing below those street trees).

What about Legality?

Having led foraging tours in city parks for decades, the question of legality comes up often. And the answer changes depending on the year, the parks commissioner, and the exact location.

For example, in the 1970s, the Central Park Conservancy published a book that not only helped people identify wild edibles in the park but also gave recipes for those wild edibles featured in the book. But unfortunately, as of this writing, it is technically forbidden to forage in Central Park. No explicit law against foraging is on the books, but laws against "damaging Park property" and "carrying gardening tools in the Park" and "taking anything from the Park out of the Park" effectively make it impossible to forage there with legal impunity. That's quite a shift in the official take on foraging.

Back in the 1980s, fellow foraging instructor Wildman Steve Brill was first arrested for foraging in the Park, then hired by the parks department to teach foraging, then quit because a new administration wanted him to stop teaching foraging. See what I mean when I say that the answer to whether urban foraging is legal changes depending on the time and the place? Although I'm completely behind parks protecting their green spaces and property, it is ironic that most of the edible plants in urban parks are invasive species that volunteers are instructed to weed out. If you want a guaranteed, 100 percent legal way to forage in city parks, volunteer for a weeding day (yes, I have done this). They will give you cool tools to work with, tell you which plants they want you to go after, and by the end of a couple of good-deed volunteer hours you'll be able to take home pounds of burdock root or bushels of garlic mustard.

Some parks do use chemical fertilizers and rodenticides. Usually these are spread only in small areas at a time with brightly colored signs or flags to alert you when these chemicals have been recently applied. But it is always a good idea to check the park's website or send an inquiry to officials to ask about their spraying practices. And remember that spraying that is citywide, such as is sometimes done to try to eliminate disease-carrying mosquitoes, takes place in parks as well.

In state and national parks, foraging is sometimes explicitly forbidden. But some state and national parks have allowable quotas, such as two pints of wild blueberries per day per hiker. Do some research before you head to these locations to find out what is officially permissible.

If foraging on private property, always ask for permission first. Most often the property owner will be happy to let you take the mulberries that are staining their pavement, the "annoying" black walnuts, the dandelions in their lawn. Do be sure to also ask whether they use herbicides, fungicides, or pesticides on their property. If they do, give that location a pass.

What about Sustainability?

One part of the issue of legality is concern about sustainability. How many people can gather a certain wild food from a location before the ecosystem suffers? Doesn't foraging deprive wildlife of food? And doesn't it threaten the continuation of the species you are harvesting? Critical to answering these questions, and to foraging responsibly, is understanding the difference between invasive and non-invasive species, as well as native and non-native plants.

Invasive, Native, and Non-Native Species

"Do no harm" should be your motto when you head out to gather wild edibles, but there's a learning curve you need to get under your belt before you can apply that motto. Understanding the difference between invasive and non-invasive species is the beginning of what you need to know in order to forage in an environmentally beneficial way.

In North America, a native plant is usually defined as any plant that was already growing on the continent before the European colonists arrived over 500 years ago. A non-native (or "alien") plant was introduced to the continent post-colonization. An invasive plant is what most people think of as a "weed." It may be non-native or native. These are extremely successful species. They grow where no one planted them without irrigation or fertilizer and usually take over the neighborhood. It is not uncommon, for example, to see a former community garden become a mugwort (*Artemisia vulgaris*) monoculture if the garden gets shut down and the gardeners can't continue their weeding.

Usually it is non-native species that end up becoming invasive. (Native invasive exceptions include pokeweed [*Phytolacca americana*] and peppergrass [*Lepidium*].) In North America, good examples of invasive non-native species are plantain, Queen Anne's lace (wild carrot—yes, it's the same plant), garlic mustard, Japanese knotweed, and mugwort. All these species were introduced from Europe or Asia and frequently crowd out slower-growing native species. In their home habitats, some of these plants are not especially invasive. For example, a British friend tells me that mugwort is not considered invasive there. On the other hand, I have seen goldenrod (*Solidago*), a native North American species, taking over whole hillsides in France.

Many slower-growing native wild edibles can't compete with invasive non-native species. Slow-to-spread wild ginger (*Asarum canadense*), for example, and plants that are easy to kill by incorrect harvesting methods such as ostrich fiddlehead fern (*Matteuccia struthiopteris*) should be harvested cautiously if at all. Research how to harvest them without killing the plant or harvest only where the species is abundant and then only a small percentage of what you find. And it is almost always a good idea to harvest by grazing, taking a little from this plant here, a little from one over there, never decimating a single plant or patch. Harvesting techniques, an important component of sustainable foraging, are covered in the individual wild ingredient sections that make up most of this book.

With invasive species, native or non-native, "have at" is a good general harvesting approach. Be aware that even small chunks of some perennial taproots such as dandelion's will regenerate into new plants if left in the earth. As will the few tiny field garlic (*Allium vineale*) bulbs you accidentally leave in the ground when you dig up a clump. Or that chip of a Jerusalem artichoke (*Helianthus tuberosus*) or a daylily (*Hemerocallis fulva*) tuber. If you're harvesting the seeds of an invasive species such as garlic mustard, it's easy to spread around just as many as you gather (see the seeds section of chapter 10 for instructions on how *not* to do that!).

The point being that it is sometimes almost impossible *not* to spread invasive species when you harvest no matter how careful you are. But you certainly don't need to worry about overharvesting these plants.

Feral vs. Wild

The dandelion is a great example of why I say that the word "weed" is not a botanical term but rather a fashion statement. *Taraxacum officinale* (dandelion) is a European plant that at different times in its history of interaction with humans has been both a treasured crop and a hated garden weed. Lawn owners still drench their properties in herbicides trying to eradicate it, even as their children make wishes while they blow on the fluffy seed heads. Meanwhile, chefs and foodies rediscovered dandelion greens years ago and they are now a common (and pricey) inclusion on restaurant menus and at farmers' markets.

Is the dandelion a weed or a choice edible? That really depends on the year you ask that question. Like dozens of other introduced plants, *Taraxacum officinale* has been in North America for centuries, through eras of being desired and eras of being detested. So when does dandelion get its green card? How many years on North American soil before we acknowledge that this incredibly useful edible and medicinal plant is here to stay (whether some like it or not)?

The dandelion was originally brought to North America from Europe as an intentional crop, and then went feral. Other feral edibles include fruit trees that pop up where a picnicker tossed a pit after gobbling the juicy pulp of a peach, or where asparagus hopped the garden fence. I define feral edibles as those that were originally planted intentionally by humans but have since spread without human direction.

And what about trees such as ginkgo and crabapple, planted by landscapers as ornamentals but offering excellent food to those in the know? Do these count as "wild" foods? Or are they also a kind of "feral"? Perhaps "underutilized" is a better way to describe them.

WILD FOODS AS PART OF YOUR BALANCED DIET

I often get asked, "What percentage of your diet is wild food?" And I do not have a straightforward answer to that question. Sometimes, my meal may be mostly wild food. Other times it may be mostly garden-grown or from my farmers' market or even the supermarket, with a few foraged ingredients thrown in. What is consistent is that every day at least some foraged ingredients find their way into what I eat.

This combination of food sources is how most traditional cultures utilize wild foods: as just one part of their diet. It may be a major part but not the only part. There would also be foods that had been cultivated, and foods that were bought or traded for. Here is an interesting point to bring up the next time someone says that industrial agriculture is the only way to feed the growing human population: Monsanto and other industrial agriculture companies say that their toxic farming methods are necessary in order to provide enough food for the ever-increasing number of humans on the planet. But if you look at which plants the herbicides they make are designed to kill, 80 percent of them are nutritious and delectable edibles such as chickweed, purslane, and lamb's quarters.

You see how the emperor has no clothes, right? "It is necessary to use our chemicals to destroy food so that we can grow enough food" doesn't really make sense.

THE DIFFERENT TYPES OF FORAGING

One thing I've learned from decades of teaching foraging is that people come to the topic for diverse reasons, all of them valid. Here are some of the different reasons that people forage.

The Lost-in-the-Woods Scenario

If you did find yourself lost in the woods (or fields or wetlands), some foraging know-how could help keep you alive. It's important knowledge to have, but this is not how traditional cultures eat.

Indigenous people do not get lost in the woods and then simply wander around and hope they find food. It's not how humans have historically fed themselves. Instead, the traditional way is to be intimately familiar with your landscape and its seasons and weather patterns. Armed with that knowledge, you are super-efficient at knowing which wild edible to look for when and where.

But okay, your foraging skills could help you out if you're ever in that lost-in-the-woods scenario. And that is important cultural knowledge to preserve and pass on. I admit I do glance at any new-to-me landscape and immediately make mental note of the wild foods I recognize. That gives me a baseline sense of security that little else matches.

Re-Wilding: The Twenty-First-Century Hunter-Gatherer

Even nomadic hunter-gatherers, maybe especially nomadic hunter-gatherers, don't just wander out into a landscape and hope to find food. Instead, they follow the food. Their migratory routes pause at the fruit trees when the fruit is ripe, at the nut trees when those are in season. And meanwhile they've got a little honey and dried root flour tied to their belts to go with whatever plant and animal foods they score on their route. This fits in with what I said above about the lost-in-the-woods scenario.

Although being able to identify and harvest wild edibles is essential knowledge for those looking to "re-wild" (as the movement to learn so-called primitive skills is sometimes called), it is important to understand that foraging did not exist in a vacuum.

The Gourmet Forager

Quite a few restaurant chefs attend my foraging workshops. They are looking for wild ingredients that they cannot find from any supplier or at any market. They want to tantalize their customers with seasonal treats such as ramps, morels, and black raspberries.

You don't have to be a professional chef to love foraging for this reason. Part of the thrill of whipping up some black walnut ice cream or a peppergrass chermoula is that I know I'm unlikely to find it at any store or restaurant (unless the chef took a foraging workshop). Although I celebrate and encourage foraging for the sake of unique ingredients, we gourmet food enthusiasts should pause and consider the impact of our enthusiasm.

Some ingredients such as fiddleheads (ostrich fern, *Matteuccia struthiopteris*) and, more notoriously, ramps (*Allium tricoccum*) are overharvested to the point of endangerment in some regions because of the allure of wild, seasonal treats. So don't order that endangered wild ingredient until you find out that it was, in fact, sustainably harvested (just by asking you will be encouraging that restaurant to make only purchases of sustainably harvested wild ingredients). Better yet, get out there and do your own sustainable harvesting.

The Traditional Forager

In cultures around the world, foraged foods are calmly included in daily meals without much fanfare. The mainstay may be grown in gardens or on farms, but there will be blackberries from the hedgerow tossed onto the pancakes when they are in season, bolete mushrooms in your risotto in autumn, acorns as mainstay or famine food depending on the decade (or century). In this scenario, wild foods take their place amid cultivated and purchased fare as one piece of the jigsaw puzzle that is a sustainable food system.

The Twenty-First-Century Forager

Since you are reading this book, you will be foraging in the twenty-first century. This absolutely includes the jigsaw puzzle of the traditional, historical sustainable food system that combines wild and cultivated foods, and of the gourmet and survivalist interests of the present era. But it also takes into account the impact our food choices have on the environment. That impact exists whether the food is wild or cultivated.

A twenty-first-century forager can have a positive or negative impact on the ecosystem they harvest from depending on (1) their harvesting methods, (2) their knowledge of invasive vs. slower growing plants, and (3) their respect for the ecosystem as primary (more important than their need for a tasty, conversation-starting dinner ingredient).

I once had the opportunity to be part of a community garden for almost a decade. When I joined, there were not enough members to keep up with the weeds, and the Japanese knotweed and mugwort (both edible and medicinal, but both highly invasive non-native species) had basically taken over the garden. We left a border of the knotweed and mugwort between us and a parking lot, partly as a boundary and partly because we just couldn't keep up with it. But over the next few years, as we persistently weeded out (and ate) the invasives from our cultivated plots, they stopped being so invasive. The weeding became less arduous. Native "weeds" such as goldenrod and pokeweed started to appear where they had had no presence before. A balance was achieved between the plants we were deliberately cultivating, and the wild plants we weeded out but also utilized. It is possible for humans to be participants in, rather than disruptors, of the places we inhabit, the places that give us life.

Another aspect of foraging is what some people now call "re-wilding." Long before that term was coined, those of us who were already teaching wild edible plant skills knew that the benefits of foraging included much more than

GETTING YOUR WILD EDIBLES HOME

FIELD DRESS

To "field dress" a wild edible means to clean it up as much as possible *before* you get it home or back to camp. Even if you can't fully wash and scrub your harvest, you can still do certain things that will make preparing the food infinitely easier later.

Brush off, or use a small knife to pare off, as much dirt as possible from root vegetables before putting them into your bag or container. Remove yellowed or browned leaves and leave them on the ground (they will compost). Shake off as much insects or debris as possible.

When you know you are going to be out in the field for hours, maybe days, before you can prepare or preserve the wild ingredients you're gathering, it is essential to know how to keep them as fresh as possible. For the most part, that information is included in the harvesting sections for each ingredient type (leaves, roots, berries, etc.). However, some tips apply to more than one ingredient type and so I am including them here.

DAMP BAG METHOD FOR LEAVES AND FLOWERS

Most wild ingredients that wilt quickly—such as delicate leaves and flowers—will hold up for at least a few hours if you use this method:

1. Remember to bring a few cloth bags such as muslin produce bags with you on your foraging foray (you can make your own from old, clean pillowcases).
2. When you are about to start harvesting your leaves or flowers, first soak your bags with some of your drinking water, or by misting the bag with water from a spray bottle. Wring out the bag so that it is damp but not dripping wet. Place the leaves or flowers directly into the damp bag as you harvest them.
3. Tie the bag to your belt or knapsack or anywhere else it will get good air circulation. The air circulation is important because it is the refrigeration created by evaporation that keeps your leaves and flowers fresh. In an arid region, you will get more of the refrigeration effect because of rapid evaporation but may need to spritz the bag with water again if your foray goes on for a long time. In humid climates, you won't get as much refrigeration effect, but on the plus side you probably won't need to dampen the bag as often.

A cloth bag plus a little water help keep greens and flowers fresh until you can get them home.

TOWEL AND BAG METHOD FOR LEAVES AND FLOWERS

This method works well for a couple of hours in the field, or several days in the refrigerator:

1. Wet a paper towel or a small piece of cloth (such as a cloth napkin). Squeeze out as much liquid as you can.
2. Put the dampened towel or cloth into a plastic bag along with your clean greens and flowers. Loosely tie the bag.

LET THEM BREATHE

Unlike leaves and flowers, which can hold up in plastic bags or containers for a few hours, mushrooms and roots may get slimy and start to deteriorate if carried this way. It is better to transport these in paper or cloth bags, baskets, or anything that provides some air circulation.

putting free food on the table, such as the sense of connection to place, to season, and to other species. On a practical level, re-wilding is a skill set that includes not merely knowing how to recognize a wild edible but where and when to look for it. But it is more than that. It is a sense of security that cannot be replaced by any fence or bank account. It is a sense of my place within the ecosystems that sustain me.

FORAGING WITH CHILDREN

When foraging with kids, the key is to get them excited about being outside on a quest for wild foods. The first step is to sit down with them to plan which wild foods to search for that are in season right then, as well as what specific ecosystems they can be found in. For example, cattails only grow in wet soil and the shoots are ready to gather in spring. From this information, you can work with them to create a foraging map and calendar for finding and harvesting the promised treasures. The map and calendar can include those wild edibles that are not in season yet but that the children can come back for when there are better odds of finding them. When gathering those wild foods that are in season on that day, encourage them to figure out whether the ingredient in question is invasive or endangered and whether there is a special, sustainable way to harvest it.

This may seem like a simple, fun game designed to keep the kids entertained. Indeed, it is fun (in a lifetime of foraging I have yet to tire of the treasure hunt aspect). But more than that, it is a game changer. After finding wild foods, kids will never experience the world in quite the same way as they did before they foraged.

Every time an informed forager begins to harvest a meal is an opportunity to benefit rather than deplete that ecosystem. This book is meant to help you become that informed twenty-first-century forager.

3

GEARING UP

YOU PROBABLY DON'T NEED nearly as much foraging gear as you think you do, but having the right tools for the job can make you a much more efficient forager. That is true not only for harvesting but also when processing your wild foods once you get them home.

A few years ago I had the chance to take a foraging workshop with a few Druze women in the Middle East. They brought no bags or containers with them. Their only tools were table knives. They wore long dresses and head scarves, and I'm sure I saw one of them give my multi-pocketed cargo shorts and leather-sheathed, cro-van steel knife a disapproving stare. These ladies harvested enough spiky thistle rosettes to eventually feed a dozen workshop participants in less than 10 minutes, using their skirts as baskets. So, yeah, you don't *need* much in the way of gear. But unless you have the crazy impressive skills those Druze ladies displayed (I don't, but I'm working on it), you'll likely want to follow some of my recommendations.

Part of deciding what gear to bring into the field depends on where your "field" is. One forager I know goes out with a huge primitive-style basket backpack, a Kay-Bar knife in a sheath at one hip, and a collapsible shovel strapped to his belt on the other side. That's great, but I can't imagine wearing such gear while trying to remain inconspicuous foraging in a city park. In addition to choosing gear suitable for your intended foraging task and potential unexpected foraging opportunities, make sure it is appropriate to your foraging landscape.

THE BASICS

This "gear" is the protective stuff that you wear to make your foraging experience more pleasant . . . or at least so that you don't get home sunburned, scratched, dehydrated, and itchy. I recommend bringing a wide-brimmed hat to keep the sun off your face (maybe one that has a functional flap of perforated material for the back of your neck) along with sunscreen, insect repellant, and a filled water bottle.

BAGS AND CONTAINERS

More essential than knives or any other tool, an experienced forager never leaves home without at least a couple of bags or containers. Even if you aren't planning to forage that day, you might unexpectedly find a wild edible that it would break your heart to leave behind. Are you really going to go home without any of those black raspberries just because you don't have anything to put them in (okay, you could sacrifice your shirt—there would be stains). Always be prepared with bags and containers on your person. I've been known to tuck a foraging bag into my fancy purse when going to an outdoor wedding because hey, you never know!

Solid-sided containers are important for berry and other fruit harvests that could easily get smashed in a bag. Baskets are great but sometimes unwieldly. The large backpack-like baskets work beautifully but may be too conspicuous depending on your foraging location. A *blickey* is an open-topped container attached to your waist that leaves both of your hands free for gathering.

I like to carry something with solid sides, such as a plastic container or basket, and two kinds of bags. Plastic bags are fine for many wild harvests if you know that you will get them processed soon. But cloth bags such as muslin produce bags or clean pillowcases are better for mushrooms and anything that you won't get around to processing for at least 4 hours (see Damp Bag Method, page 14).

Odds are you aren't going out in an ankle-length dress like those Druze ladies, but thank them for the reminder that in a pinch a hat or an overshirt can be sacrificed if you forgot your containers at home.

KNIVES

After bags and containers, a knife is arguably the most useful tool a forager can carry into the field. But what makes an awesome foraging knife?

The truth is that it depends on what you're harvesting. A small pocket knife will make it easier to snap off sprigs of *Monarda* and *Melilotus* than if you tried to do the same deed by hand. A sturdier, mid-sized knife is useful for tasks such as cambium harvests and immature-but-thick burdock flower stalks. An even bigger knife can be more useful than a shovel or digging stick to jostle out a root that is in hard-packed soil. I own, and use, all the above.

The two medium knives will work for most foraging jobs, but the others come in handy in certain circumstances.

Harvesting wild garlic using a knuckle knife.

DIGGING TOOLS

When your intended harvest is a root, it's obvious that you've gotta dig. And just as obviously, you need something to dig with.

Collapsible shovels are a good option if you need something you can carry in a knapsack. I find trowels less useful because they can't dig deep enough to get at some deep underground harvests such as burdock taproots.

A digging stick is an ancient and still-reliable way of digging. Find a sturdy stick about 1½ to 2 inches in diameter. Shave off one end to a spade-like point. The height doesn't actually matter so long as it is not too short—you should be able to stand upright or only slightly bent over while working with it.

A dirt knife is any large, extremely sturdy knife (it needn't be particularly sharp) that you don't mind plunging into the soil and jimmying around the root. You don't want to accidentally slice your intended harvest into pieces, so you should use the dirt knife to loosen the dirt at least 2 inches away from where the plant enters the ground.

A shovel is a useful foraging tool, but not the only way to unearth edible root vegetables.

My favorite way to dig up stubbornly embedded root veggies is to use a one-two punch of first loosening up the soil around the plant with a large, sturdy knife or a digging stick, then jostling out the root by jimmying a trowel or shovel around it.

The last and most important digging tool is patience. Once you've got the soil around a root loosened to a good depth (what a "good depth" is depends on the length of the root you are trying to harvest), start jiggling the root by hand, loosening its grip on the soil. Don't sharply bend or yank on the root until the soil around it is sufficiently loosened or the root will snap, leaving a good portion of your intended harvest still in the ground.

GLOVES

I don't carry gloves with me as a rule (she said, ducking to avoid the derision of fellow foragers who do). The trouble with gloves is that I can't feel what I'm doing as sensitively as I can bare-handed: it's harder to sense the approaching snap point of a shoot, or pluck a flower, or even twist off a bunch of chickweed without mangling the stems. But they sometimes come in handy, such as protecting the hand pulling the prickly brambleberry canes toward me while the other (bare and able to sense what it is doing) hand picks the berries. For such situations, I just use sturdy garden or work gloves.

THE NUT WIZARD

While not mandatory, a Nut Wizard is an immensely useful tool in late summer and early fall. You simply hold the long handle and roll the basket over black walnuts, windfall apples, and other solid, fallen tree crops. The Nut Wizard scoops them up, making it easy to transfer the harvest to a barrel or bucket.

▶ This gadget makes picking up treefall nuts (black walnut, butternut, etc.) and windfall fruits such as apples super easy.

4

WHICH WILD EDIBLE
WHERE AND WHEN

TIMING AND LOCATION are just as important as leaf shape or the color of the flower when it comes to finding and identifying wild edibles. This chapter includes all the plants, mushrooms, and seaweed mentioned in the book, organized by what time of year to look for them and in what kind of terrain. Although this book is intended more as a guide to foraging technique than a field guide, some wild edibles are featured with field guide–style plant profiles; those plants are boldfaced in the following lists.

EARLY SPRING

From a forager's point of view, "spring" is two seasons, not one. What goes into a forager's collection basket in early spring is utterly different from what you'll find just a few weeks later. For that reason, early and mid-spring have separate listings.

Early spring is peak harvest time for many greens such as dock, dandelion, and chicory that will become extremely bitter once the weather gets balmier. It is also still a good time to harvest roots and rhizomes that will soon be fibrous and depleted as biennial and perennial plants use up the starch they've stored underground to fuel spring's burst of growth. And finally, early spring offers a welcome burst of color as well as flavor with flowers including violets and redbud blossoms.

FIELDS, DISTURBED SOILS, SUNNY AREAS, AND EDGES OF SUNNY AREAS

basswood (linden) leaves
    and inner bark
birch sap and inner bark
broad-leaved and curly dock leaves
burdock root
cat's ear
chickweed
chicory leaves and roots
dandelion leaves, crowns, and roots
daylily shoots
evening primrose leaves and roots
garlic mustard greens
Japanese knotweed shoots
Jerusalem artichoke
juniper
meadow mushroom
milk thistle
mint
mugwort
nettles

plantain leaves
redbud blossoms
sassafras bark and roots
thistle roots
violet leaves and flowers
wild asparagus shoots
wild carrot roots and leaves
wild garlics including field garlic
    and Neapolitan garlic

WOODLANDS AND PARTIALLY SHADED PLACES

basswood leaves
birch sap and inner bark
chickweed
clearweed
daylily shoots
garlic mustard leaves and roots
goutweed
granulated slippery jack mushroom
Japanese knotweed shoots
mint
nettles

WOODLANDS AND PARTIALLY SHADED PLACES (*continued*)

ostrich fern
oyster mushroom
ramps
redbud blossoms
sassafras bark and roots
shagbark hickory bark
slippery elm bark
spicebush twigs
spruce tips
turkey tail mushroom
violet leaves and flowers
**wild garlics including field garlic
    and ramps**
wild ginger
yarrow

SEASHORE AND COASTAL AREAS

dulse
juniper

WETLANDS, RIVERBANKS, LAKESIDES, BOGS

birch inner bark
cattail shoots and lateral rhizomes
clearweed

MID-SPRING TO LATE SPRING

By mid-spring the landscape even in urban places has exploded with the colors of flowers and a thousand shades of green. Some of those flowers are good eats. And while the rosette leaves and roots of early spring may no longer be choice, this part of the season brings shoots and flower stalks, immature flower heads, and the first ripe fruits of the year.

FIELDS, DISTURBED SOILS, SUNNY AREAS, AND EDGES OF SUNNY AREAS

amaranth greens
anise hyssop
Asiatic dayflower
basswood blossoms
bee balm
black locust flowers
broad-leaved and curly dock
    flower stalks
**burdock roots and immature
    flower stalks**
chickweed
chicory roots
common mallow
dandelion flowers and roots
daylily buds
elderberry flowers
evening primrose leaves
fennel leaves and stalks
grape leaves

honeysuckle
juneberries
juniper
lamb's quarters greens
lilac
milk thistle
milkweed florets
mint
mugwort
mulberries
nettles
northern bayberry
peppergrass
pineappleweed
plantain young leaves
pokeweed shoots

purslane
quickweed
red clover blossoms
sassafras leaves, bark, and roots
Siberian elm samaras
sow thistle leaves and shoots
sweet fern
thistle shoots
wild asparagus shoots
wild carrot leaves and roots
wild grape leaves
wisteria flowers
wood nettle
wood sorrel
yarrow

WOODLANDS AND PARTIALLY SHADED PLACES

basswood blossoms
birch inner bark
chickweed
clearweed
elderberry flowers
garlic mustard greens, flowers, and immature seedpods
goutweed
juneberries
oyster mushroom
sassafras leaves, bark, and roots
shagbark hickory bark
Siberian elm samaras
slippery elm bark
spicebush leaves
spruce tips
turkey tail mushroom
violet young leaves
wild ginger
wood nettle
wood sorrel

SEASHORE AND COASTAL AREAS

dulse and other seaweeds
juniper
northern bayberry

WETLANDS, RIVERBANKS, LAKE-SIDES, BOGS

angelica
birch inner bark
cattail shoots and rhizomes
clearweed
jewelweed

SUMMER

Summertime and the foraging's easy. There are plenty of mild-flavored leafy greens, such as lamb's quarters, in abundance. The parade of seasonal fruits from plums to brambleberries offers fresh colors and flavors every week. You'll find summer mushrooms, too, and toward summer's end the first nut crops of the year.

FIELDS, DISTURBED SOILS, SUNNY AREAS, AND EDGES OF SUNNY AREAS

amaranth leaves
anise hyssop
Asiatic dayflower
bee balm
black cherry
blueberry
brambleberries
burdock
butternut
chickweed
chicory roots
common mallow
Cornelian cherry
dandelion roots
daylily buds and flowers
elderberry fruit
evening primrose seed
fennel pollen
garlic mustard seeds
goldenrod
grape leaves and fruit
hawthorn
jewelweed
juniper
lamb's quarters greens
magnolia buds

FIELDS, DISTURBED SOILS, SUNNY AREAS, AND EDGES OF SUNNY AREAS (continued)

melilot
milk thistle
milkweed florets and pods
mint
mugwort
mulberry
northern bayberry
oxeye daisy
pear
peppergrass
pineappleweed
plantain young leaves and seeds
prickly pear
purslane
quickweed
red clover
rose leaves and flowers
sassafras leaves, roots, and bark
sumac
sweet fern
thistle roots
wild American plum
wild carrot flowers and seeds
wild peach
wood sorrel
yarrow

WOODLANDS AND PARTIALLY SHADED PLACES

Asiatic dayflower
black cherry
blueberry

brambleberries
chicken of the woods mushroom
chickweed
clearweed
Cornelian cherry
elderberry fruit
garlic mustard seeds
grape leaves
hawthorn
honewort
magnolia buds
mint
oak acorns
oyster mushroom
sassafras leaves, bark, and roots
shagbark hickory bark
slippery elm bark
spicebush leaves and twigs
turkey tail mushroom
wild ginger
wood sorrel

SEASHORE AND COASTAL AREAS

beach plum
dulse and other seaweeds
juniper
northern bayberry

WETLANDS, RIVERBANKS, LAKESIDES, BOGS

birch inner bark
cattail pollen and immature seed heads
clearweed
jewelweed

FALL

In autumn the fruit harvests continue with tree fruits including wild apples and silverberry. Nut season reaches its peak, and you'll be racing the squirrels and other wildlife to that bounty. Leaf and root crops come back into season, some like dandelion even giving up the bitter edge they had in summer. And early fall is glory time for some of the choicest wild edible mushrooms on the planet.

FIELDS, DISTURBED SOILS, SUNNY AREAS, AND EDGES OF SUNNY AREAS

amaranth seeds
American hazelnut
apple
Asiatic dayflower
black walnut
broad-leaved and curly dock
butternut

chickweed
chicory roots and leaves
crabapple
dandelion roots
daylily tubers
evening primrose roots
field garlic
ginkgo
goldenrod
grapes

FIELDS, DISTURBED SOILS, SUNNY AREAS, AND EDGES OF SUNNY AREAS (*continued*)

hawthorn
Jerusalem artichoke
juniper
lamb's quarters seeds
magnolia buds
mallow
meadow mushroom
mint
northern bayberry
oak acorns
pear
quickweed
rose hips
sassafras bark and roots
silverberry
sweet fern
thistle roots
wild carrot leaves and roots
wild grapes
yarrow

WOODLANDS AND PARTIALLY SHADED PLACES

American hazelnut
birch inner bark and twigs
black walnut
butternut
chicken of the woods mushroom
chickweed
garlic mustard roots and leaves
hawthorn fruit
hickory nuts

honewort
lion's mane mushroom
magnolia buds
oak/acorn
oyster mushroom
sassafras bark and roots
shagbark hickory bark
silverberry
slippery elm bark
spicebush berries and twigs
turkey tail mushroom
wild ginger

SEASHORE AND COASTAL AREAS

dulse and other seaweeds
juniper
northern bayberry

WETLANDS, RIVERBANKS, LAKESIDES, BOGS

birch inner bark and twigs
jewelweed
mint

WINTER

It ain't over until . . . well, it's never really over when it comes to foraging. In some areas such as California, winter is the peak foraging season, when rains restore the hills from parched gold grass to lush carpets of edible greens and mushrooms. Even in areas locked in snow and ice, there are still fruits such as rose hips that are tastier after a few freezes, and edible barks. Most seaweeds are at their tastiest when the waters they grow in are chilly (time to pull on those warm, thigh-high fisherman's boots). In late winter, sap-tapping season begins, and the sweetness of that wild product is a harbinger of spring.

FIELDS, DISTURBED SOILS, SUNNY AREAS, AND EDGES OF SUNNY AREAS

chickweed
crabapple
evening primrose roots and rosette leaves
hawthorn fruit
Jerusalem artichoke
juniper
magnolia buds
rose hips
sassafras bark and roots
thistle roots
wild carrot roots

WOODLANDS AND PARTIALLY SHADED PLACES

basswood bark
birch inner bark, twigs, sap
chickweed
field garlic
granulated slippery jack

honewort seeds
magnolia buds
maple sap
oyster mushroom
pine bark
sassafras bark and roots
shagbark hickory bark
slippery elm bark
spicebush twigs
turkey tail mushroom

SEASHORE AND COASTAL AREAS

dulse and other seaweeds
juniper

WETLANDS, RIVERBANKS, LAKESIDES, BOGS

birch inner bark, twigs, sap
cattail rhizomes

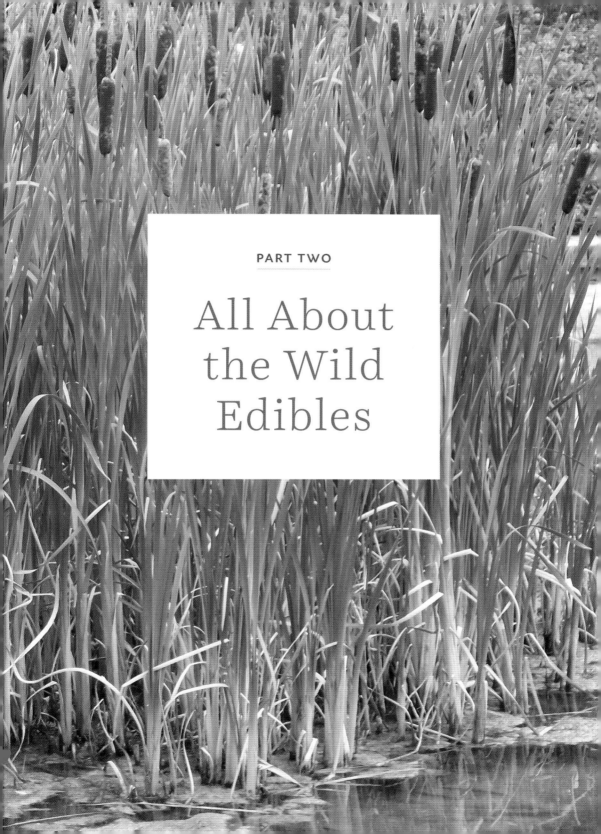

PART TWO

All About the Wild Edibles

5

LEAVES

OF ALL THE FABULOUS wild foods out there, leaves are arguably the most under-appreciated and the most important. Foragers are quick to post brag photos equivalent to hunters' trophy shots of morels (a highly sought-after spring mushroom) or a fat score of ripe beach plums, but they tend to be ho-hum about leaves. Yet leaves are what foragers eat a lot of during most of the year. Whether served raw in a salad or cooked with a little garlic into a tasty "mess o," greens are by far the most abundant wild food.

Edible leaves are available year-round in many places, some even emerging from snow cover during brief winter thaws. They come from trees, shrubs, and

Lamb's quarters, amaranth, pokeweed, and lady's thumb are all abundant in this patch of delectable green.

low-growing plants of both annuals and perennials. In many cultures, wild leafy greens are symbolic of the end of winter and the beginning of three seasons of warmth and abundance. My own Greek relatives still get a sparkle in their eye when a steaming dish of *horta* (Greek for any hodgepodge of wild edible greens) is on the table.

Some wild edible leaves are the everyday invasive edible plants that a forager finds frequently. I call these "the usual suspects": dock, lamb's quarters, garlic mustard, dandelion, chicory, purslane, chickweed, etc. Others are more herb than vegetable, to use a cook's terminology. These are seasonings used in small amounts to bring vibrant flavor and aroma to your dishes. Examples include sassafras leaves (use in gumbo as a thickening agent and to add a tingly taste) and spicebush leaves for summer iced tea blends.

While we are chasing those springtime-only morels and hoping we hit the timing just right for those beach plums, there are almost certainly wild edible leaves at our feet that can provide a base and some bulk for our next wild foods dinner. Instead of pasta or rice, try a salad of violet and redbud leaves or a mess of sautéed garlic mustard greens as the base for other ingredients and sauce. Now clearly wild greens can provide the bulk but not the calories of starchy foods like root vegetables and grains. And in centuries past, that might have been a downside. But let's face it, for most twenty-first-century humans in Western cultures, the problem is not too few calories but too many.

Edible leaves are some of the healthiest vegetables available, wild or not wild. They are usually high in fiber, and the wild ones often have higher nutrient values than their cultivated counterparts. Although leaves may not contribute many calories, they are so nutrient-rich and readily available that they should be considered the forager's mainstay. Wild greens are loaded with antioxidants and phytonutrients. In general, domesticated vegetables have been bred for bulk and blandness (think iceberg lettuce). Wild greens often have stronger flavors than we are used to, and those intense tastes are signs of alkaloids, essential oils, and other compounds that often carry health benefits. That bit of bitterness you taste in your wild greens is doing your body good.

This chapter is a guide to the broad categories of wild greens that will be available to you three or—depending where you live—possibly even all four seasons of the year. General harvesting methods for leaves are covered under the individual type of leafy green in this section. Does it grow in a rosette, a branching pattern on green stems, or on a tree? In terms of preparing leaves, most edible leafy greens can be eaten raw or cooked. See the introductory section for details on dealing with leaves that are a little too chewy, bitter, fuzzy, or otherwise technically edible but not yet good. Preserve leafy greens by blanching and freezing, or by dehydrating. Aromatic leaves can be dried and crumbled into seasoning blends. You can also lacto-ferment them into wild kimchi.

These abundant greens will nourish you, satisfy your taste buds, and are probably outside your door right now. Please treasure them as much as you treasure the "sexier" but less generous wild foods that are only in season for a few weeks.

LEAVES THAT GROW IN A ROSETTE PATTERN

If the leaves are the main attraction, and if those leaves are growing in a rosette pattern, this section will help you work with them efficiently and deliciously. Plants with edible leaf rosettes are valuable to the forager because they can be easier to harvest in quantity than leaves in other growth arrangements.

What does it mean to have leaves growing in a rosette pattern? It means that the leaves grow in a circular pattern, attaching to the root at a central point. You are already familiar with some of these plants from the supermarket. Leafy vegetables that grow in "heads"—lettuce, cabbage, and endive—are all examples of rosettes. Picture a head of romaine lettuce: Are the leaves growing along a stem? No. They have no stems, and the leaves are all attached at a central point. That is a leaf rosette.

This first-year evening primrose plant has both edible leaves and roots. You can harvest this one even in winter during thaws.

Remember that not all plants with edible leaves that grow in a rosette pattern have edible roots, and so the following method is *not* suitable for those with inedible roots. (An example is common blue violet, *Viola sororia*, which has edible leaves, stems, and flowers, but toxic roots.)

Check your field guide (website, book, or instructor) and confirm that the plant you've found and are interested in harvesting has both edible leaves in a rosette pattern *and* edible roots. These plants usually also have edible flowers (covered in chapter 8).

Some plants, such as the perennial dandelion, *only* grow leaves in a rosette, never sending up a branching stem of any kind. Others, such as burdock and evening primrose, are biennials that grow their leaves in rosettes during their first year, but then shoot up a flower stalk with leaves growing from it the following spring.

This is the traditional way to harvest edible leaves that grow in a rosette pattern and are connected by a sliver of edible root.

DANDELION (*Taraxacum officinale*)

FIND AND IDENTIFY

Look for dandelion in full to partial sunlight, especially in disturbed soil areas such as lawns, gardens, farms, parks, urban lots, and even cracks in the sidewalk.

The dandelion is one of the few wild plants that even city dwellers can usually identify. What kid hasn't blown on a fluffy dandelion seed head? Growing in a rosette, dandelion leaves have sharply and irregularly toothed margins (the name dandelion comes from the French *dents de lion*, or "teeth of the lion"). The points of the "teeth" face straight out or back toward the leaf base, which is not true of plants that look similar. The bright yellow flowers emerge from the center of the plant on leafless stalks. When cut or broken, the plant exudes a milky sap, which is often used to treat warts. The slender taproot of this originally European plant is brown on the outside and grayish white on the inside.

Dandelion leaves all attach to the roots at a central point, forming a circular rosette. This much-maligned "weed" provides at least three edible parts and is also a prized herbal medicine.

Dandelion has no poisonous look-alikes, although chicory (*Cichorium intybus*) and cat's ear (*Hypochaeris radicata*) have similarly shaped leaves that also grow in rosettes. But unlike dandelion, chicory's branching stalks bear blue flowers, and cat's ear plants are hairy. Chicory and cat's ear also have edible roots, leaves, and flowers.

HARVEST

Because it is so common, I like to use dandelion to demonstrate the best technique for harvesting plants that have both edible leaves growing in a rosette pattern *and* edible roots. This traditional method has been used around the world for many hundreds of years because it is extremely efficient: you can gather the entire leaf rosette in just a few seconds, rather than wasting time picking one leaf at a time. It also gives you a more substantial vegetable because the crown where the leaves join the root and new leaves emerge is heftier than the leaves by themselves.

Slide one hand (or foot) under all of the leaves on one side of the leaf rosette. Fold those leaves over the ones on the other side of the rosette. Slip a knife just below the soil surface and slice sideways, severing just the top sliver(s) of root. In just a few seconds, you have harvested the entire rosette of leaves.

PREPARE

"Yard squid" is what I call leaf rosettes harvested in their entirety. They have an intriguing mix of textures from the tender leaves to the chewier roots and crowns, and a flavor that is savory and faintly bitter (in a good way). The sliver of edible root holds together the leaves, and if the plant is young and the leaves small the result can look like a circle of tentacles (think calamari). Sauté these whole small rosettes in a little butter, oil, or

◁ "Yard squid" is a description for early spring dandelion rosettes that I learned from forager Melana Hiatt. They do look a bit like calamari when fried tempura-style.

bacon fat; steam or boil them; or (my favorite) make yard squid tempura by dipping the whole rosette in tempura batter and frying it.

Dandelion Crowns

The "crowns" of edible leaf rosettes from plants that also have edible roots are arguably the tastiest part. The crown is simply the top sliver of root and the bases of the attached leaves plus any nascent flower buds nestled down in the center of the rosette. Gather the leaves of a rosette you've harvested in one hand while with using the other hand to slice just above the sliver of root. Set the leaves aside for another use. What's left is the crown.

A dandelion crown is a vegetable that is both substantial and tender. As long as the leaves aren't too bitter to be palatable, the crowns will taste good. You can use almost any cooking method including stir-fry, steam, boil, and bake. Cook the crowns until tender, then eat them on their own, bake into a casserole, serve on pasta or rice, or employ in any way you would a delicious cooked vegetable.

Dandelion Leaves

You can use edible leaves that grow in a rosette pattern in exactly the same ways as edible leaves that grow in other arrangements. Whether they are best raw or cooked depends on the individual species and also the time of year at which they were harvested. For example, early spring dandelion leaves are great in salads, but as the weather warms up they become a bit more bitter and may need a pre-blanching to be palatable. Just like cultivated greens, wild edible leaves shrink so much during cooking that it takes a big bunch of leaves to equal a few small portions of the cooked vegetable. For example, you'll need as much as 10 cups of raw dandelion leaves to yield 1 cup of cooked dandelion.

Dandelion Roots

Although outside the leaf rosette topic, it's important to know that dandelion roots are both edible and medicinal. The best time to harvest dandelion root for its medicinal benefits (digestive aid, liver ally, diuretic that does not deplete potassium the way synthetic diuretics do) is when the whole plant has become too bitter to taste good to most people (usually during summer's warmest months).

You can chop up fresh dandelion roots and add them to soups. You can also chop, roast, and grind them, then brew them like coffee: the hot beverage has a great molasses-like taste and is used by herbalists as a tonic for the digestive system, liver, and kidneys. The roots are best preserved by chopping them and then roasting in a 300°F oven until they are completely dry and chocolate brown. Be sure to chop before roasting because whole dried dandelion roots are very hard and difficult to break into small pieces or grind.

Dandelion Flowers

Chop dandelion's sunshine-colored flowers and add them to omelets (I leave the green calyxes on for this), or (petals only) baked goods, pancakes, and fritters. You can also preserve the essence of dandelion's roots, leaves, and flowers by making beer or wine from them.

PRESERVE

Blanching and then freezing is the best method of preserving whole leaf rosettes attached to a sliver of their edible roots. You can also use this method to freeze the leaves and crowns separately. Dehydrating is also a good option for the leaves, which you can then crumble into soups, stews, stuffings, and fillings throughout the year. Note that dehydrating doesn't work as well with the crowns because the thick bit of root and the thin leaves have very different drying times.

PLANTS WITH EDIBLE LEAF ROSETTES BUT INEDIBLE ROOTS

Most edible wild plants whose leaves grow in a rosette pattern also have edible roots, but there are exceptions. If a plant has edible leaves but a poisonous root, clearly you don't want to include a sliver of that root in your dinner. Therefore, this calls for different **harvesting** methods.

You could use the method described above that *does* include keeping the leaves attached to a bit of the root, but then cutting away the bit of root before proceeding with your recipe for the leaves. Or try this method: Gather the entire rosette of leaves in one fist as if it were a bouquet. Use scissors, a knife, or pruners to cut the leaf bases or stalks just above the soil level (and—important!—below your hand that is holding the leaf rosette together). Have a bag or container ready to receive the now-separated leaves.

COMMON BLUE VIOLET (*Viola sororia*)

The showy flowers of shade-loving violets are lovely to look at in early spring. But while the edible purple flowers may catch your eye, the mild, lettuce-flavored leaves are also good to eat and have a longer harvest season than the flowers. Use them in spring and summer as salad, soup thickener, and a cough remedy.

FIND AND IDENTIFY

Violets can tolerate full sun but are usually found growing in partial shade. They prefer moist soil and thrive under deciduous trees where they make the most of the early spring sunlight coming through the still winter-bare branches. Later in the year, the plants get relief from hot summer sunshine when the trees they are growing under leaf out.

Learn to identify violet leaves so that you can recognize the plants even when they are not in flower. The heart-shaped leaves grow in a rosette. They

Wild violets provide pretty and mild-flavored leaves, flowers, and flower stalks (which, by the way, taste different from the flowers and leaves). The roots, however, are inedible.

have fine teeth along the margins and pointed tips. When the flowers aren't present, novice foragers sometimes confuse violets with garlic mustard, which likes similar shady, disturbed soil situations and also has a basal rosette of heart-shaped leaves. But a violet leaf's tip is sharply pointed as are the tiny teeth on the margins, whereas garlic mustard's basal leaves have scalloped, rounder edges. The shades of green are different, too, as are the venation patterns (turn a violet leaf over and you'll clearly see the prominent veins, especially in bigger leaves). But really all you have to do is use your nose: garlic mustard leaves smell like garlic and mustard, whereas violet leaves don't really have a smell.

Young violet leaves are curled in on themselves like scrolls rolled in from both sides. This is the ideal stage to harvest them. The first flowers that wild violets produce in early spring are the showy ones that are so pretty on salads. They are usually purple with some white near the center, but sometimes they are mostly white. These sterile flowers are about ¾ inch in diameter and grow on narrow leafless stalks that can be several inches long. There are five petals on these flowers, and the side petals have white hairs at their bases.

In summer, violets produce self-pollinating, petal-less flowers that you probably won't notice. These become three-parted capsules that eject the small round seeds. Violet roots are knobby, branching, somewhat horizontal rhizomes. They are not edible.

HARVEST

Collect wild violet's purple or purple-and-white flowers at any time during the early spring flowering season. Pinch them off with their long, thin flower stalks attached as these are also tasty. These showy flowers are sterile and you are not endangering the plant by harvesting them. In any case, violets are tough and prolific to the point of being invasive, so sustainability is not an issue when you harvest any part of them.

The leaves are good spring through summer. As the plants mature, it is best to harvest only the smaller, partially furled leaves as the bigger leaves can get tough and stringy. Violets are perennial plants that will regenerate from the inedible root that you leave in the ground.

PREPARE

Violet leaves, flowers, and flower stalks are all mild and delicious raw in salads. The flower stalks have a subtly different, sweeter flavor than the leaves and flowers, so these really should be treated as three different ingredients. The leaves never get bitter, but the veins of older violet leaves can be tough and stringy. Use young leaves raw, but dry or bake the older leaves into chips (see Leaf Chips recipe on page 249).

Cooked fresh violet leaves are a bit slimy. That may sound unpleasant, but they act as a binder when added to veggie burgers, and they are good for thickening soups and stews.

PRESERVE

Candy the flowers to preserve them, and then use them as dessert decorations. You can also make a beautifully colored syrup with the flowers. You can dry the leaves to save for winter use. Crumbled into soups, dried violet leaves are a good thickening agent. They also have a reputation as a soothing tea for coughs and chest colds.

LEAVES WITH A MAT-LIKE GROWTH HABIT

Some excellent leafy wild vegetables including chickweed (*Stellaria*), purslane (*Portulaca oleracea*), and wood sorrel (*Oxalis*) are low-growing plants that form mat-like patches. Often the leaves are small, and picking these plants one leaf or even leaf tip cluster at a time is way too laborious for the food you get. But yanking up whole handfuls of them by the roots will leave you with a lot of dirt and stringy roots in your bag.

There are two better ways to **harvest** leaves with a mat-like growth habit: the haircut method or the twist technique (described on page 48). These efficient gathering methods will also encourage more lush growth in the plants. Some of you are looking at me sideways right now because you've spent hours yanking out these annoying garden weeds. But while I, too, weed around my tomatoes and other cultivated plants, I also "cultivate" plants such as wild chickweed. Harvest chickweed with these methods, and you can collect from your favorite patch again and again.

COMMON CHICKWEED (*Stellaria media*)

FIND AND IDENTIFY

Although chickweed will grow in full sun and even dry-ish soil, in those conditions it will hug the ground and its stems will be tough and stringy. That is *not* the state in which you want to harvest it. Instead, look for chickweed in moist soil and a part-shade, part-sunlight situation. It is a common farm, park, and garden weed.

Chickweed prefers cool weather, and in areas with mild winters you can gather it fall through spring. It often dies back where summer gets intensely hot, but even then you can sometimes find it in semi-shaded spots.

Even in the cushiest growing conditions, chickweed is a low-growing plant with slender stems. Its leaves join the stems in pairs (called an "opposite" leave arrangement) and are usually less than an inch long, sometimes much less. The leaves have smooth margins and pointed tips on an otherwise oval shape.

Common chickweed's green flower buds dangle on slim stems, looking a bit like earrings. The small flowers are only about ⅛ inch in diameter. At first glance it looks like there are ten diminutive white petals, but a closer examination reveals that there are only five petals but each one is deeply cleft into a V.

Unlike other (also edible but less tasty) chickweeds, *Stellaria media* has the unique characteristic of a single line of hairs running up its stems. Not hairy stems, mind you, but just that single line of hairs, which you can clearly see with a magnifying lens or even just by holding a sprig of common chickweed up in sunlight.

> **WARNING** Some novice foragers confuse poisonous spotted spurge (*Euphorbia maculata*) with chickweed (and with purslane, *Portulaca oleracea*). There's an easy and quick way to make sure you've got the safe plant: Look at the stems you just cut or twisted off. Spotted spurge stems will ooze a white latex; chickweed and purslane stems will not.

▶ Common chickweed is a mild green that is excellent both raw and cooked and is available three or in some places even four seasons of the year.

HARVEST

All the aboveground parts of chickweed are edible (use common sense to decide whether the stems of the plants you've found are tender enough to be good eats). Harvest chickweed using either the haircut method or the twist technique.

To harvest these leaves with the haircut method, gather up a bunch of the low-growing plant into a bouquet in one fist. With your other hand, use scissors or pruners to cut across the bunch of stems just below your fist. Your "bouquet" is now freed from the growing plant, and ready to put into your collection container.

Almost as efficient is the twist method. Found a terrific patch of wood sorrel or chickweed but don't have scissors or pruners on you? Not to worry. Gather a fistful of stems in one hand. With your other hand, twist the tops of the plants until they snap off.

Stellaria media is an invasive species introduced to North America from Europe. There are no sustainability issues around gathering it. However, if you want to be able to harvest from a favorite patch again and again during its growing season, be sure to harvest just the top few inches and leave the roots in the ground.

PREPARE

Common chickweed is excellent raw in salads or in place of lettuce in sandwiches, as well as briefly steamed, boiled, or sautéed. You can also use it in pesto, but remember that it is not aromatic like basil or other cultivated herbs commonly used in pesto.

Note that chickweed contains saponins, and if you are one of those people who is genetically sensitive to saponins (you probably hate cilantro), then you won't like chickweed. But most people will find it pleasantly mild and green-tasting.

PRESERVE

Blanch and freeze chickweed greens (and any flowers that happen to be on them).

This method of harvesting results in lusher subsequent harvests, and less dirt in your collection bag than if you had just yanked the plants up.

No knife or scissors handy? No problem. With many soft-stemmed—but too thin to snap— wild edibles, a simple twist will do the trick.

LEAVES ON BRANCHING, NON-WOODY STEMS

These are plants with leaves that join the herbaceous (non-woody) stems in one of the following arrangements: alternate (one leaf at a time), opposite (leaves attaching to the stems in pairs), or whorls (leaves attaching in a circle like a ballerina's tutu). Numerous choice wild greens are in this category, including Asiatic dayflower (*Commelina communis*), quickweed (*Galinsoga parviflora*), and lamb's quarters (*Chenopodium album*).

Unlike leaves that grow in rosettes, which often become too bitter to taste good during summer, leaves on branching, non-woody stems can be mild-flavored spring through fall. This makes them a valuable resource for the forager's table.

When you **harvest** these leaves in spring, you can often include the tender stems too. As spring turns into summer, the stems will often become tough and fibrous even though the leaves may still be tender with good flavor.

Preparing these leaves is easy. You can use them cooked or raw. Let your taste buds guide you as to whether the texture of the leaves you've gathered is appropriate raw in a salad or better cooked. Steaming, stir-frying, and simmering are all good ways to prepare mild leafy greens. Add a little seasoning of your choice and enjoy hot or at room temperature. Or add your cooked greens to soups, omelets, and other dishes.

As with other wild edible leaves, blanching and freezing is the best way to **preserve** these leafy greens. But you can also dehydrate them to add a nutritional boost to winter soups and stews.

LAMB'S QUARTERS (*Chenopodium album*)

FIND AND IDENTIFY

Also called wild spinach, and in some regions goosefoot, lamb's quarters is a common weed that loves full sun and the frequently turned-over soil of gardens, farms, parks, and roadsides.

I've heard two explanations for the common name lamb's quarters: one is that the triangular shape of the leaves looks vaguely like a lamb's nuzzle seen from above, with the point of the triangle being the nose and the back two points the ears. The other explanation, which I find more debatable, likens the shape of the leaf to the upper haunches of a lamb's leg.

Lamb's quarters gives foragers two wild foods: mild-flavored and fine-textured leaves as well as edible seeds that are similar to quinoa.

Although it's a forager's cliché to say that a wild edible leaf tastes "like spinach," lamb's quarter's mild flavor and silky texture (once cooked) really does. The first two "true" leaves on the plant join the stem in an opposite arrangement, but after that the leaves grow in an alternate arrangement, each leaf joining the stem farther along than the previous leaf.

The leaves, especially the younger leaves near the tips of the branching stems, are coated with a distinctive whitish coating that you can rub off. Lamb's quarters does not have a noticeable scent. Most of the leaves are triangular with softly toothed margins, but the upper leaves of older plants that are flowering and going to seed will be smaller and elliptical. The branching stems are often grooved and frequently have some magenta coloration.

Lamb's quarters flowers are small and green; they grow in branching clusters. The small black seeds are also edible.

HARVEST

Chenopodium album is a widespread and invasive plant, and there are no sustainability issues around harvesting it. Be especially careful that the site you gather from is not highly polluted—this is one of several plants that tends to accumulate the chemicals and heavy metals of industrially farmed and urban locations.

The general leaf harvesting method on page 48 works great for lamb's quarters. The important thing to remember is that although all the aboveground parts of the plant are edible, some are better than others. You can harvest the leaves can by pinching them off anytime, but you'll get the most food for your effort if you harvest the entire tips, leaves, and tender stems together. In mid-spring and early summer, you may be able to use as much as the top 8 inches of the plant. Once the plants start to flower, the stems become too fibrous to bother with. And the green flowers are not particularly palatable. At this stage I usually move on to other wild edibles and come back to lamb's quarters when the seeds are ripe. See the small seeds section on page 151 for the best methods for harvesting lamb's quarters seeds.

PREPARE

You can eat the leaves and tender stalks of lamb's quarters raw, but I think they are much better cooked (steamed, boiled, or stir-fried). Once cooked, lamb's quarters is excellent in omelets, ravioli and other pasta dishes, dips, and more—use your imagination. As with spinach and other tender leafy vegetables, lamb's quarters loses a lot of bulk when cooked. Figure about 10 cups of chopped, raw lamb's quarters leaves and stems if you want to end up with 1 cup of cooked.

The seeds can be cooked in place of quinoa in recipes and can also be ground into flour or used whole in baked goods.

PRESERVE
As with other mild, leafy greens, you can blanch and freeze lamb's quarters. The seeds will keep in a dark, dry place for several months.

AROMATIC LEAVES

Aromatic leaves are the secret seasoning in your roast recipe, the intriguing taste in your herbal infusion, the kick in your salad dressing. In cook's vocabulary, they are commonly called "herbs." They are rarely eaten in quantity by themselves but rather used to season blander ingredients. It is worth doing a little research into the medicinal uses of these plants, because the same essential oils that give them their aroma and taste invariably have medicinal properties as well.

Aromatic leaves grow on plants of diverse shapes—from trees and shrubs such as sassafras (*Sassafras albidum*), California bay (*Umbellularia californica*), northern bayberry (*Myrica pensylvanica* syn. *Morella pensylvanica*), and spicebush (*Lindera benzoin*), to lower-growing plants such as yarrow (*Achillea millefolium*), sweet fern (*Comptonia peregrina*), or epazote (*Dysphania ambrosioides*).

Most aromatic leaves grow in alternate (joining the stems singly) or opposite (joining the stems in pairs) leaf arrangements, so the harvesting method is very straightforward. Always **harvest** from the tips of the stems or branches. You can go back several leaf nodes, but it is better for the plant to include the active growth tips in your harvest rather than denuding the stem of leaves below the tip. This is because of the principle of apical dominance, which means that so long as the growth nodes at the tip of a plant (or branch of a plant) are intact, the other growth nodes farther back along the plant remain dormant. You know what I mean if you've ever picked the bottom leaves off of a basil plant and ended up with what I call a basil palm tree: a long, leafless stem with a tuft of leaves on top.

Spicebush is a shrub native to northeastern North America that is usually prized for its fruits and twigs. But its leaves make a fabulous cold-infusion tea in the summer, with a taste that is both citrusy and floral.

But when you harvest from the tips and ends of this type of plant, those dormant growth nodes farther back along the stems wake up. The plant branches out, creating a bushier, more robust plant *and* more leaves for you to harvest.

The simplest method of **preparing** aromatic leaves is to make a tea-like infusion by steeping the leaves in hot water. It is important to cover the pot, cup, or bowl during the steeping time so that the aromatic oils don't evaporate. You can also use aromatic leaves as culinary herbs by adding them directly to food. Tender leaves such as mint (*Mentha*) and bee balm (*Monarda fistulosa, M. didyma*) can be minced and added at the last minute to recipes. More leathery leaves including bayberry, California bay, and sweet fern can be added whole during cooking to impart flavor, and then removed before serving.

You can easily **preserve** most fragrant leaves by drying. Remember that the essential oils that flavor the leaves are volatile and evaporate when exposed to heat. For this reason, I do not recommend using a dehydrator to dry aromatic plants, not even on the lowest setting. Instead, bundle the stem ends of several

Yarrow's leaves and flowers have a taste reminiscent of sage and make an excellent savory seasoning. They also have a long history of use as a medicinal herb that disinfects wounds and helps stop bleeding.

sprigs with a rubber band, and hang the bundle somewhere away from direct light and heat for 1 week. Depending on your climate, at the end of the week they may be dry enough to crumble off the stems or twigs and transfer to storage containers.

If your climate is humid, even after a week the leaves may not be dry enough to crumble off easily. In this case, turn your oven on to its lowest setting for 10 minutes to preheat. Turn the oven off. Place the mostly dried herbs in a heatproof bowl and put the bowl into the cooling oven for no longer than 5 minutes. Let the leaves cool completely at room temperature before transferring them to storage containers.

Another method of preserving aromatic leaves is to first extract their flavor in an infusion, and then strain the infusion into ice cube trays. Freeze the cubes and then transfer them to freezer bags or containers. This is the best method for preserving the flavor of spicebush leaves, which do not keep their aroma when dried.

BEE BALM (*Monarda fistulosa*, *M. didyma*)

FIND AND IDENTIFY

Monarda didyma loves full sun, but *M. fistulosa* is somewhat shade tolerant and grows alongside woodland paths and clearings. As the common name suggests, bee balm flowers are big-time pollinator attractors and are often planted in butterfly gardens for that reason. Bee balm is a perennial native to the Americas that dies back to the ground each winter and regrows from the root in spring.

Like other plants in the mint family (Lamiaceae), bee balm has square stems and leaves that join the stems in pairs (an opposite leaf arrangement). The leaves have toothed margins. The first time most people see a *Monarda* flower head, they mistake it for a single flower. It is actually a cluster of small flowers that are each fused into a tube at the base. *Monarda didyma* flowers are red to magenta, whereas *M. fistulosa* flowers are pale lavender. Numerous stamens project out of each flower tube, and the overall effect of the flower head is like a wacky explosion from a Dr. Seuss book.

Both bee balm's leaves and flowers are richly aromatic with a scent and taste like a fruity oregano. And, as the common name suggests, it is a major pollinator attractor.

HARVEST

Gather bee balm in summer when it is just beginning to bloom. In most locations, as soon as peak bloom season is past the leaves will start to be coated with powdery mildew. This isn't dangerous, but I would not deliberately add it to my stew. Try to harvest before white spots appear on the leaves. Pinch or snip off the top few inches of the stems, leaving the lower leaves to photosynthesize.

PREPARE

Use bee balm fresh or dried as a flavoring herb in savory dishes, or infused for a hot beverage. The flavor varies from one species of *Monarda* to another: *M. fistulosa* has a light citrus taste, while *M. didyma* tastes more like oregano.

PRESERVE

In addition to drying well using the general method for aromatic leaves, you can steep bee balm leaves (and flowers) in vinegar for 1 to 4 weeks. Strain out the herbs and use the fragrant vinegar in salad dressings and marinades. Bee balm is also an excellent candidate for an herbal seasoning salt. Combine 4 parts (by volume) minced leaves with 1 part sea, kosher, or other non-iodized medium-grain salt.

EDIBLE TREE LEAVES

In spring, the newly emerging leaves of many trees are not only safe to eat but delicious too. These include basswood or linden (*Tilia*), birch (*Betula*), mulberry (*Morus*), slippery elm (*Ulmus*), redbud (*Cercis*), and maple (*Acer*). Keeping in mind (important!) that not all trees and shrubs have edible leaves, here's what to look for on the ones that do.

The choicest edible tree leaves will be shiny, bronze-tinted, and translucent. Within days of unfurling they will be matte rather than shiny, green, opaque, and no longer as good to eat. When you **harvest** edible tree leaves, never strip off all the leaves on a single branch. Not only is this unsightly for the next passerby, but if you left the apical node intact (tip growth) then the branch will not fully leaf out again, ever. Instead, you could pluck off just the cluster of leaves at the end of the branch. This will encourage the dormant growth nodes on the branch to wake up and produce more leaves. Or you could look for the glossiest, most translucent leaves on each branch and gather some but not all of those. Move from branch to branch, grazing, always leaving more leaves than you take.

In theory, you could blanch and freeze edible tree leaves to **preserve** them, but in my experience they are best used fresh and raw in salads or as wraps for spring rolls.

REDBUD (*Cercis* species)

FIND AND IDENTIFY

You're more likely to find redbuds, also known as Judas trees, growing where landscapers planted them than wild, and most of the time those landscapers had no idea there was anything edible about them.

Redbuds are small trees that rarely reach their potential maximum height of 30 feet. They sometimes form multiple trunks, making them more shrub than tree-like. The branches often grow in a funny zigzag pattern, an effect that is amplified when the trunks grow in corkscrew turns (not present on all redbuds, but common). Young redbud bark is smooth but will be scaly and cracked on older trees.

Redbud flowers may be hot pink or, less commonly, white, and the flowers appear on the branches before the leaves. Redbud blossoms also appear well before most other trees or shrubs have broken winter dormancy, making them easy to spot even from a distance. The flowers grow in clusters that look like they are growing directly from the branches. Each flower in a cluster is approximately ½ inch long, and looks like pea or bean flowers (they are all members of the legume family, Fabaceae).

There will still be some flower clusters on the tree when the leaves first appear. The leaves are heart-shaped with smooth margins. They grow in an alternate pattern on the branches, and have petioles that are swollen at both ends.

In late spring and early summer, redbuds produce flat, 2- to 4-inch seedpods that look like snowpeas and eventually turn chocolate brown.

HARVEST

Redbuds have edible flowers, leaves, and seedpods that appear in that order. To harvest the flowers, which taste delightfully like lemony green beans, simply twist off entire clusters. This does not harm the tree, but think about the

This photo of edible redbud tree leaves (*Cercis*) shows clearly two leaves of similar size at the best-to-eat stage (on the right) and the past-yummiest stage (on the left).

Better known for its green bean–flavored pink flowers that stand out in the early spring landscape, redbud trees also have delicate, delicious edible leaves.

person who will be there after you and refrain from denuding an entire branch. Graze instead, taking a cluster from one branch, then another. The delicious leaves are often neglected even by experienced foragers. Use the general harvesting method outlined on page 57. Harvest the seedpods very early into their growth cycle before they get stringy. If they don't snap in half easily with a simple twist, they're already too far gone to bother collecting.

PREPARE

Use the young leaves raw in salads (my preference) or cooked. Sometimes you'll find large leaves that are still in the choice stage despite their size; these are terrific to use instead of rice wraps for summer rolls. The flowers are excellent raw, pickled, in frozen desserts, or added to muffins and other baked goods. The young seedpods are good raw, cooked (steamed, boiled, stir-fried), or pickled.

PRESERVE

Although the young leaves can technically be blanched and frozen, they are much better when used fresh in season. Redbud flowers keep in the refrigerator for up to one week and indefinitely when pickled. The young seedpods can be blanched and frozen.

CONIFER NEEDLES

The evergreen needles of pine (*Pinus*), juniper (*Juniperus*), fir (*Abies*), and spruce (*Picea*) are aromatic, packed with vitamin C, and worthy inclusions in the forager's pantry. Used as a seasoning more than a main bulk ingredient, conifer needles are aromatic and bring bright flavors that can be citrusy, pleasantly resinous (when used sparingly), and, well, piney. Conifers have a long history of use as flavorings, from the pine-flavored Greek wine Retsina to the juniper used to give gin its distinctive taste.

To **harvest** edible evergreen tips, in spring, look for tufts of new-growth needles on the ends of conifer branches. They will be a far lighter green than the older needles farther back on the branches. Called "candles," these tufts of new growth are much less bitter and much more aromatic than the older foliage.

Harvest the candles when you are ready to use them soon (their flavor rapidly declines even when refrigerated) by snapping or snipping them off

WARNING Not every tree or shrub with evergreen, needlelike foliage is edible. Yew (*Taxus*) foliage is toxic. Stick to pine, juniper, fir, and spruce species, and always take the time to compare your plant samples with a good field guide.

halfway down. In this way you are gathering only the choicest new growth but also leaving some of the candle on the plant to continue its new growth (this is also standard pruning practice for conifers).

The texture of conifer needles, even the young ones on the candles, isn't as fabulous as the flavor. To get around the texture, **prepare** them by mincing or pulverizing the needles so finely that their texture is almost imperceptible, or extract their flavor into another medium and then strain out the actual needles.

Edible conifer needles make excellent tea, syrup, sorbet, vinegar, flavored sugars and salts, and alcoholic extractions (spruce beer is a classic). Many of the most beloved recipes for preparing conifer needles are also ways to **preserve** their flavors year-round. I don't think they are worth drying because they lose so much of their flavor when dehydrated.

SPRUCE (*Picea* species)

FIND AND IDENTIFY

Look for spruce trees in boreal (coniferous) forests throughout the Northern Hemisphere. They are also frequently planted by landscapers, so you may see them in parks and gardens well outside of their natural range.

Spruce trees are in the same plant family as pines (Pinaceae) and like pines they have seed-bearing cones. However, their needles are much shorter and are not gathered in bundles like many pines. Rather, spruce needles attach singly via a swollen area called a pulvinus, which remains behind when a needle drops to the earth. The pulvini are arranged in whorls on the branches. If you slice a spruce needle in half, you will see that the cross-section is triangular or square rather than round. Spruce trees usually grow in a cone-like (think stereotypical Christmas tree) shape.

HARVEST

Follow the general harvesting method instructions for conifer needles to gather spruce foliage (see page 60).

PREPARE

Young spruce needles infuse refreshing flavor into any liquid (vinegar, syrup, honey, alcohol, water), sugar, or salt base. To make spruce sugar or salt, combine 4 parts (by volume) finely minced fresh spruce needles with 1 part sugar or salt. These condiments will last almost indefinitely. Use the infused sugar to flavor desserts and cocktails, and the salt for roasted vegetables, seafood, and pork. If you are a homebrewer, you're probably already aware of spruce beer. But simply infusing the candles in vodka will yield an interesting mixology ingredient.

PRESERVE

All the ways I mentioned to prepare spruce needles are also ways to preserve them.

▶ Young spruce tips add a slightly citrusy, slightly resinous seasoning to diverse recipes from beer to sorbet.

6

ROOTS, TUBERS, RHIZOMES, AND BULBS

WARNING Underground roots and rhizomes often tangle together into nearly indistinguishable parts. Once you're familiar with the edible underground part you're looking for, it will be easy to avoid the dangerous ones it may be entwined with. But remember the forager's rule: *If in doubt, leave it out*. And always follow a plant all the way from its aerial parts to its roots to confirm its ID.

Burdock taproots are cultivated in Japan as the vegetable *gobo*, but they're just starting to catch on at some farmers' markets in North America. The wild roots usually have a much earthier, more complex taste than the cultivated ones.

HORSERADISH-SPICY GARLIC MUSTARD ROOTS, hearty Jerusalem artichoke tubers, invasive-but-delicious field garlic—these are but a few of the tasty treats that fall into this category of wild edibles. Anyone who has tucked into a burdock root stir-fry or a glazed evening primrose root side dish can attest to how delicious and filling wild roots can be.

When we eat these underground harvests, we are taking advantage of the sugars and starches that the plants were storing to prepare for the next cycle of growth. Let's say you're a Jerusalem artichoke a.k.a. sunchoke (*Helianthus tuberosus*). Your aerial parts are going to die down to the ground for winter. Then comes spring, and you need to grow some new leaves and start photosynthesizing ASAP. But here's the catch: it takes energy to produce leaves—energy that is produced by photosynthesis—and coming out of winter dormancy, you don't have any leaves to do photosynthesis. Yikes. But if last year, when you did have leaves, you stashed some of the carbohydrates you were producing through photosynthesis in your underground tubers, all is well. Come spring, you simply spend those carbohydrate reserves to create new leaves.

First, let's talk about **harvesting** sustainably. You might think that when you dig up the underground parts of a plant you are more likely to kill it than when you harvest any other plant part. That is sometimes true, but not always. Some underground plant parts are capable of regenerating and growing a new plant. Examples include dandelion and ramps. Others are not: even if you leave some of the root in the ground an evening primrose or burdock plant will not grow back.

Wild roots sometimes have a tougher or more fibrous texture than cultivated ones but great flavor. The way to get the flavor without the dubious texture is to finely chop, mince, or (once cooked) purée them. These **preparation** methods make the most of the flavor and nutrition in wild roots, while getting around the sometimes-tough texture. You can also use them as soup stock flavorings. Successfully **preserve** all wild roots, tubers, rhizomes, and bulbs by dehydrating or pickling them. Canning, however, results in a mushy, less-tasty product. Wild bulbs freeze well. Starchy roots, rhizomes, and tubers do not, turning mushy or grainy even when they are blanched or otherwise cooked before freezing.

TAPROOTS, TUBERS, RHIZOMES, AND BULBS

What's the difference between these? All these plant parts grow underground and are easy to lump together as "root vegetables." But knowing a bit about their differences botanically will help you understand what makes one harvesting method more sustainable than another.

A taproot is a primary root, growing straight down if growing conditions permit, from which secondary rootlets may grow.

A tuber is a modified stem that grows straight down.

A rhizome is a modified stem that grows horizontally.

A bulb is made up of layers of modified leaves.

TAPROOTS

A carrot is the quintessential taproot. Carrots and other taproots are roots that are thickened by the starches they store. They reach straight down into the soil (or try to; a rock or other obstruction can make a taproot bend or fork away from the typical carrot shape). The top of the taproot where the leaves emerge is usually wider than the bottom, which typically tapers to a pointy tip.

Many biennials including wild carrot (Queen Anne's lace), evening primrose, and burdock have carrot-shaped taproots. When you dig up a taproot you are digging up the whole plant, and in the case of biennials—which are some of the best edible taproots—this does kill the plant. Fortunately, edible biennial taproots tend to be invasive species, so you are doing an environmental good deed when you **harvest** them. With perennials such as dandelion, it's a different story. Even a small piece of the root left in the soil can regenerate into a new plant (as any lawn owner can verify). These plants are frequently invasive, so harvesting them can be an environmental good deed.

Wild taproots are good **prepared** in most of the same ways as cultivated roots: in soups and stews, cooked then mashed, roasted, or shredded and added to quick breads, muffins (think carrot bread), or veggie burgers. Dandelion and chicory roots can also be roasted and brewed into a caffeine-free, coffee-like beverage.

To **preserve**, know that taproots dehydrate well. They are also good candidates for finely chopped or grated pickle recipes such as vinegar brine–based relish or lacto-fermented wild kimchi.

EVENING PRIMROSE (*Oenothera biennis*)

FIND AND IDENTIFY

Native to North America, evening primrose has five edible parts (taproot, leaves, shoots, flowers, and seeds). It loves disturbed soil and full sun situations, and it's a common weed in urban and suburban settings.

Evening primrose is a biennial, meaning that the plants that germinate from seed one year will not flower and then go to seed until the following calendrical year. So-called "first-year plants" are ground-hugging rosettes that you can spot (and harvest) even in the middle of winter. The lance-shaped leaves in the rosettes have mostly smooth margins and are up to 5 inches long, with a distinctive white midrib that is sometimes pink-hued near the base of the leaf. Brush away some of the soil from the plant's base, and you'll see that the top of the root also has pink coloration. The rest of the taproot is beige to light brown.

In spring or early summer, depending on location, "second-year" evening primrose plants (those that germinated in the previous year) will shoot up 3- to 5-foot-tall flower stalks. Eventually, the flowers will open their four bright yellow petals. Later in the growing season, these plants produce narrow seed-pod capsules between ½ and 1 inch long. As these pods start to mature and turn brown, the tips split and flare out.

In addition to its radish-flavored taproot, evening primrose leaves, flowers, and seeds are also edible.

HARVEST

Evening primrose taproots are best eaten before the plants start to send up a flower stalk. This means that they are at their peak from fall through early spring. They have a bit of a radish-y bite, which can be intriguing from a culinary standpoint. Dig them up anytime the soil isn't frozen by circling around the leaf rosette with a shovel or dirt knife, and then jiggle the taproot out.

Harvest the leaves anytime, and the shoots before the plants flower—when you've just started to see some taller stalks shooting up from the basal leaf rosettes. The flowers are edible but wilt quickly, so harvest as close to eating as possible. The seeds can be harvested any time after the pods turn brown.

Even where it is native, evening primrose can be invasive. Harvesting the taproots will not endanger the species. And odds are good that when you harvest the seedpods you'll inadvertently spread some of the seeds around. Sustainability is not a major concern with this plant.

PREPARE

Although all parts of evening primrose are edible raw, some people find that it causes a mild throat and/or stomach irritation. I use the flowers raw in salads but prefer the leaves, shoots, and roots cooked. When cooked, the plant has a mucilaginous texture that is odd on its own but a plus when used to thicken curries, stews, and other soups. The seeds are hard on your teeth if chomped on raw, but they're tasty and gently crunchy once roasted or cooked in a dry skillet.

PRESERVE

Dehydrate evening primrose roots for future use in soups and stews. The leaves and shoots don't preserve especially well, turning from pleasantly pungent to annoyingly acrid when dried or frozen. The flowers are also best used fresh. The seeds can be stored in paper or cloth bags still in their pods for up to one year, or once winnowed kept in airtight jars for several months.

TUBERS

When **harvesting** for tubers, dig a wide and deep circle starting at least 1 foot in radius out from the main stem(s) of the individual plant. It is not unusual to dig as deep as 10 inches before you hit the first tubers with your digging tool, although usually they'll start appearing sooner.

Tubers are a forgiving harvest when it comes to sustainability: leave a chip of a Jerusalem artichoke in the ground and it will generate a new plant next year (or, in my experience, a squirrel will probably dig it up and move it to a new location and then forget about it, resulting in a new J-choke location next year). Replant daylily roots with a few of the tubers still attached, and the plants will bounce back just fine.

The usual advice is to cook wild tubers like potatoes. That **preparation** advice works, if by that you mean boiled, steamed, pan fried, or roasted. Just keep in mind that the cooking time for wild tubers is often shorter than for cultivated potatoes.

Tubers can be **preserved** by dehydrating. They are not great when canned or frozen (even after blanching); no one seems to like the resulting mushy texture. They are better pickled, or dehydrated and then ground into flour.

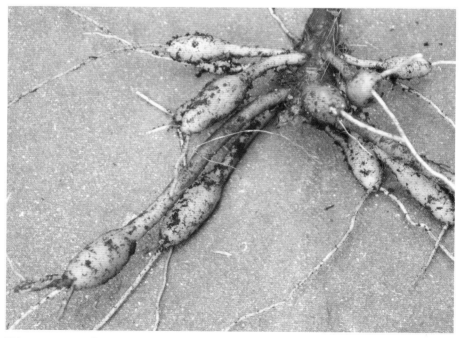

Tubers are not really roots at all but modified stems. Dig up a tuber-producing plant such as daylily or Jerusalem artichoke, and you'll find a tangled spread of underground stems with plump, starch-packed tubers attached.

DAYLILY (*Hemerocallis fulva*)

FIND AND IDENTIFY

Look for daylily in sunny and partially sunny spots. When growing wild or feral, it often appears on roadsides and the edges of fields. And of course, it is often planted in gardens.

When daylily first shoots up from its perennial roots in early spring, a novice might mistake its overlapping, untoothed leaves for poisonous iris. But iris leaves are blue-green, unlike daylily's yellow-green. More distinctively, the bases of iris leaves overlap in a flat way like a fan, whereas daylily shoot leaves cup each other with the flat sides facing each other like hands about to applaud.

As the season progresses, the leaves become long and strappy, and grow in big, floppy rosettes. The flower stalks shoot up as tall as 3 feet (although often shorter) and are leafless or at most have a couple of short leaves. This is very different from Easter and tiger lilies, which have short leaves densely arranged along their flower stalks.

Daylily's torpedo-shaped buds open into flowers with six petals (technically the petals are tepals). The orange or tawny daylily is what you will find growing feral or wild, but cultivars in many colors and even twice as many tepals are planted in gardens. Daylilies get their name from the fact that each flower only opens for one day. You are not depriving tomorrow's flower-appreciators if you pick daylily blooms in the afternoon because they wouldn't reopen the next day anyway. But a perk for foragers is that the buds open over several weeks, extending their harvest season.

Dig a daylily up, and you'll find attached to its thin but ropy roots, tubers that look something like fingerling potatoes. They range from pinkie finger to thumb size. Daylilies are perennial but not evergreen: the aerial parts of the plant die back to the ground for the winter.

HARVEST

Harvest daylily shoots in early spring when the leaves are still upright and embracing each other, and have not yet opened out and gotten long and floppy (and too tough to eat). Slice them off just above soil level. The plants will regenerate from the roots.

In late spring and summer, break off daylily flower buds anytime they are 1 inch or longer. I prefer them when they are completely green, but I know

foragers who prefer them when they are showing some orange. Daylily flowers are also edible. In fact, dried daylily flowers are sold in Chinese markets as "golden fingers" and used in soups. I prefer the texture of the tepals without the central reproductive parts of the flower, so I usually pull these apart after I've snapped off the flower by hand.

Dig up daylily tubers in fall or early spring. Sustainability is not really an issue with this potentially invasive plant, but if you want to ensure that your patch of daylilies thrives, simply replant a few of the tubers with some stringy roots attached. A great solution to finding a legal location to dig daylily tubers is to find someone who is growing them. Daylily patches need to be thinned periodically to produce the maximum amount of bloom. Offer to help with the thinning, and take some of the tubers you dig up home. But don't make this offer in summer because the tubers will be depleted then.

PREPARE
The faintly onion-flavored shoots are excellent stir-fried. The buds can be cooked like you would cook green beans (meaning that the same cooking methods and times apply, not that they taste the same). The flowers are good raw as a salad or soup ingredient or garnish. You do not need to peel the tubers before using. Simply snip off the roots, scrub them clean with a vegetable brush, and cook them using any method you would with very small potatoes.

PRESERVE
The tubers will keep in the refrigerator or another cool place for 1 to 2 weeks. The shoots can be blanched and frozen. The buds make excellent vinegar-based pickles, and they would probably be good lacto-fermented, too, but I haven't tried this. Dehydrate the flowers whole (or just the tepals); they are sweeter dried than fresh, and add a welcome dash of color to winter dishes.

RHIZOMES

Rhizomes, modified stems that spread out horizontally, are among the forager's most important foods because of the starch- and flavor-packed mass they provide. Commercially grown ginger is a familiar example of a rhizome.

◀ Daylilies are frequently planted as ornamentals but have naturalized across much of North America.

I use two sustainable **harvesting** methods with rhizomes. In the case of a colonizing wetland plant such as cattail, I usually ignore the older rhizomes (although they could yield edible starch) and focus instead on the active growth tips (see Cattail entry below). For a ground cover plant such as wild ginger (*Asarum*) I dig just a few inches below the soil, lift up the horizontal rhizomes (with the plants and threadlike roots attached), and use scissors, a knife, or pruners to snip off a section of the rhizome that is connecting two of the leafy plants. I keep the rhizome for my harvest and replant the leafy clumps that have still have plenty of roots attached. The replanted parts will shoot out new rhizomes. In this way, I can come back to the same wild ginger patch again and again without depleting it.

Preparation really depends on the rhizome in question. Some, such as wild ginger, have such a strong aroma and taste that they are best used in small amounts as a seasoning. Others, such as cattail laterals, are mild enough to use as a main vegetable ingredient. You can **preserve** edible rhizomes by drying, pickling, or blanching and freezing.

The two cattail rhizomes and growth tips on the right that have started to curve are past their prime, but the younger, un-curved rhizomes are an excellent vegetable.

WARNING Some foragers avoid wild ginger rhizomes because of potential toxicity. I use them—but sparingly—as a spice, not a vegetable. Another option is to skip wild ginger's rhizomes and use the leaves instead. You'll find more information about this plant and its edibility (or not) online in the resources.

The slow-growing rhizomes of wild ginger can be harvested without killing the plants.

CATTAIL (*Typha* species)

FIND AND IDENTIFY

Cattail species grow in shallow water or muddy ditches: in other words, they like it wet. Their light blue-green sword-shaped leaves have smooth edges. They can grow as tall as 9 feet and have been used for thatching roofs and weaving into mats and baskets. Look for cattail's dark brown "corndog" seed heads, which persist even in winter when most of the plant is dormant. These cigar-like seed heads turn from brown to fluffy white over the course of the winter.

Cattail plants have both male and female cylindrical flowers that are either on top of each other or slightly separated. It is the female flower that becomes the iconic brown seed head. Cattails grow in colonies, with the aerial parts of the plant shooting up from the horizontal rhizomes that lie in the muddy layer just below the water. Cattail rhizomes do not branch between the growth nodes from which the leaves shoot up. Older rhizomes are light brown with a solid core, spongy outer layer, and stringy roots along their length.

Cattail is easy to identify and in addition to the young lateral rhizomes provides five other edible parts.

HARVEST

Cattail provides several different edible ingredients including the hearts of the shoots, which are excellent in spring before the plants flower. Slice the shoots off near the base, cut off the green leaf tips, and then peel away the outer layers until you get to the white core that looks similar to hearts of palm. While doing this, you will notice that the cut cattail shoots exude a gel. This gel is healing for any cuts and scrapes you may get during your foraging foray.

Another edible part is the male flower heads, which can be used as a vegetable reminiscent of the baby corn in American-style Chinese food. Snap or snip these off the plants when they are still green. But leave plenty of these flower heads on the plants so that you can come back and gather the edible pollen a few weeks later. Gather the pollen by covering the flower heads with a paper bag and shaking. Note that if it has been windy recently most of the pollen will have already blown away, and you should wait a few (hopefully less windy) days for more pollen to develop before trying to harvest this golden flour.

Now about those rhizomes barely buried in the mud, plump with the starch they are storing to power the next spring's cycle of growth . . . The fact that the starch in the cattail rhizomes is meant to overwinter and be ready to serve as an energy savings account for the plants next spring clues us in as to the best time to harvest them. The rhizomes will be at their most plump and good to eat from late fall through early spring. Cattail's growth cycle also tells us that the rhizomes will be depleted and fibrous during mid-spring through mid-summer when the plants have just recently used up their energy creating new leaves and flower heads. The best time to harvest the rhizomes is in late summer after the plants have flowered through the start of the next spring.

To harvest, reach down into the shallow water and feel around in the mud. You're trying to locate a horizontal rhizome. The best ones to eat will be those that have *not* started to curve upward at the tip. Once you've confirmed whether or not you've found a nicely straight "lateral" (as some forager's call them), feel back the other direction away from the tip. Eventually, you will feel some stringy roots on the rhizome. From the growth tip back to just before you felt the stringy roots is good eats. Snap or slice off this section. Older, fibrous rhizomes can be pounded in water to release their starch, which can then be used as a thickener. In my opinion, this cattail product is more trouble than the end result is worth.

I snip the velvety brown, cigar-shaped seed heads off the plant with pruners. Harvesting a few of the shoots and rhizomes will not damage the cattail colony, which will continue to produce new rhizomes and shoots. Always leave several of the stacked male and female flowers so that the females get pollinated and produce the seed heads.

WARNING Two other wetland plants with extremely similar leaves often share habitat with cattail. Yellow flag (*Iris pseudacorus*) is poisonous but its yellow, iris-shaped flowers mark it as quite different from *Typha* species. Sweet flag (*Acorus calamus*) has a strong, spicy fragrance whereas cattail is almost scentless.

PREPARE

Peel off any brownish outer layer from the bases of young cattail rhizomes. The remainder is a mild but delicious vegetable that is good when steamed, stir-fried, and baked into casseroles. My favorite preparation is to simmer the rhizomes with butter, maple syrup, and a splash of water until the water evaporates and they are tender and lightly glazed.

The hearts of the spring shoots are good raw or cooked. Their gel makes them too slimy raw for some people but once cooked that texture is minimized. As with the rhizomes, the flavor is mild but excellent. The immature male flower "cobbs" can be steamed, boiled, or stir-fried (parboil first for the best texture). Sift cattail pollen through a fine-mesh sieve to remove any insects or debris. Do this indoors and don't sneeze—cattail pollen is a very fine powder that easily blows away. The pollen has a beautiful gold color and faintly nutty flavor. Combine it with grain flours in pancakes or any baked good. Lastly, you can pull the brown seed heads apart and cook them for a long time in a strongly flavored sauce. The punks (as the cattails are sometimes called) will develop a texture similar to barbecued pork but contribute little flavor of their own.

PRESERVE

Young cattail rhizomes can be blanched in boiling water for 2 minutes and then frozen. The shoots can also be frozen, but I find their texture suffers even when they are blanched. Store cattail pollen in airtight containers.

◀ Harvesting cattail rhizomes does involve getting wet and muddy.

BULBS

Bulbs are not really roots but layers of modified leaves with roots attached. Think about a scallion: it has some stringy roots at the bottom, then the white part, which merges directly into the green parts. In fact, both the white layers and the green parts they merge into are the leaves (the stringy things at the bottom are the real roots).

The best way to **harvest** bulbs sustainably depends on the particular species. Bulbs that can be invasive such as *Allium vineale* (field garlic) and *A. neapolitanum* (Neapolitan garlic) can be harvested freely. But bulbs that are endangered in many places (e.g., *A. tricoccum* or ramps) need to be harvested with special care. If you dig up a whole clump of ramps, for example, it can take as long as 7 years for the surrounding plants to replenish that now-barren area.

Wild Neapolitan garlic (*Allium neapolitanum*) has edible bulbs, leaves, and flowers with a much milder oniony flavor than commercial garlic.

Both fast-growing invasive bulb plants and slow-growing potentially endangered bulb plants will regenerate into a new plant if a bit of the bulb with the roots attached is left in the ground. So the first thing to do is to check a field guide and find out whether the bulb species you are harvesting is endangered in your area. If not, and especially if it is an invasive species such as field garlic, go ahead and dig it up. If it is a slow-growing species that is endangered in some regions, you need a different approach. You can simply look at the patch of bulb-producing plants you've found and take care not to harvest more than 25 percent. That is an approach that I and other foraging instructors have recommended in the past. The trouble is that foraging is increasingly popular. And if you take 25 percent, and the guy foraging for the trendy restaurant takes another 25 percent . . . well, you get my point.

There is another way, but because it takes a bit more time and attention, it isn't often used by professional foragers working for the farmers' markets and restaurants. This technique is a win-win situation that allows you to harvest bulbs without devastating the plant population you are harvesting from. Use a sturdy knife to loosen the soil around a clump of the bulbs/plant you want to harvest. Reach into the soil with your hand and feel for the bulb/root clump. Slide your knife horizontally a centimeter from where the stringy roots are attached to the bulbs. Pull out the plant you are harvesting. Pat the soil firmly down over the bits of bulbs and attached roots that your knife left behind. They will regenerate into new plants.

Preparing alliums can be as simple as adding them, raw or cooked, to jazz up a neutral base such as rice. Is there a savory recipe that *doesn't* call for an onion, garlic, leek, or shallot? They are so essential to cooking that Steven Sondheim even wrote a song that begins with the lyric "First you brown an onion." The wild counterparts of cultivated *Allium* bulbs are equally useful. Use them in every savory dish, and in pickles and relishes. Bulbs are among the easiest wild ingredients to **preserve.** All edible bulbs freeze and dehydrate well. They are also excellent pickled.

RAMPS, WILD LEEK (*Allium tricoccum*)

I hesitated before choosing ramps as the example plant for this section on bulbs. For one thing, in many places it is incorrectly harvested to the point that it is endangered. And it also has a limited range, growing only in the eastern half of North America. But stay with me, because it is a perfect example plant even if you live in a different part of the world.

FIND AND IDENTIFY

Look for clumps of this slow-growing native plant in the eastern part of North America in early spring. Although they are endangered in many places (due to overharvesting and unsustainable harvesting methods), it is still possible to come across great swaths of ramps in the Northeast. Ramps grow as a ground cover under deciduous trees. Before the leaves on the trees above them unfurl, they get plenty of direct sunshine to fuel a burst of growth. By the time the trees start to shade them out, they are already dying back to the ground, not to be seen again until the following spring. Bulb plants with this growth pattern that makes the most of the light coming through bare tree branches in early spring are called ephemerals. Other ephemeral plants include familiar cultivated ornamentals such as daffodils (which are not edible, by the way).

The leaves of ramps leaves look very similar to lily-of-the-valley leaves. They are oval, 4 to 12 inches long, and have smooth margins. The leafstalks are often purple or reddish. Unlike the inedible lily-of-the-valley, every part of ramps has an oniony smell.

The rounded umbels of small white flowers appear just as the leaves are starting to yellow and die back. They become hard black seeds that appear in groups of three, which will remain on the plant weeks or even months after the rest of the plant has disappeared for the year. Underground the purple-red leafstalks become slender, whitish, teardrop-shaped bulbs. Thin, stringy roots grow from the base of the bulb.

WARNING
Careful attention to sustainable harvesting methods is required.

▶ Sustainable harvesting methods are essential with ramps, which are endangered in some places (although abundant in others). These were correctly harvested leaving the base of the bulbs and the roots in the ground to regenerate.

All plants that smell like onions or garlic are edible. Use your nose!

HARVEST

Ramps are overharvested and endangered in some places because of the unsustainable harvesting method of digging up the entire plant over a large area of a patch of ramps. It can take up to 7 years for ramps to grow to full size from seed but only a matter of minutes to dig them up.

The main reason this unsustainable harvest technique is prevalent is because people get greedy about this prized wild ingredient. Cash greedy. Restaurant chefs love to feature it on their menus for the few weeks that ramps are available in early spring. Perhaps it is the shortness of its season as well as the lovely flavor that makes this wild food so sought after. In any case, you can make good money selling ramps to chefs. And when folks are getting paid per pound, they may not be thinking about learning better but admittedly slower harvesting techniques. If you are a chef, please ask your professional forager about their harvesting methods before you pay for their box of ramps. If you are a customer, ask before you order.

Here are the three correct ways to forage this lovely and tasty ephemeral:

1. Snip off the leaves and leafstalks, leaving the bulbs and roots in the ground intact. The aboveground parts of ramps are also delicious.

2. Hold a clump of ramps near the base with one hand. With the other hand, use a sharp knife to slice across the clump about 1 inch below soil level. What you'll get are the leaves, leafstalks, and the upper parts of the bulbs. The bases of the bulbs with their stringy roots will remain in the ground and regenerate new leaves.

These two methods work with any *Allium*, by the way. You can even regrow store-bought scallions by slicing off the white bases with attached roots and planting them.

3. If you find an especially large patch of ramps in an area where they are not endangered, go ahead and harvest some of the whole bulbs along with the other plant parts. But do this carefully, digging a small clump here, another over there, never leaving a big bald spot in the patch. If you can tell that some other forager dug in the ramps patch before you, use one of the first two methods instead.

Whichever method you use, the best time to spot and gather ramps is in early to mid-spring before the plants flower. I used to say that you could still collect the bulbs during the rest of the year by remembering where you'd found the plants in spring and also looking for the seed heads, but now I discourage that technique unless the plants are extremely abundant where you plan to dig.

PREPARE

Every part of ramps has a wonderfully gentle yet distinctive oniony taste, like leeks with attitude (and indeed, another name for ramps is wild leek). I prefer to use ramps as the star ingredient with other more neutral supporting ingredients such as rice (ramps risotto is heavenly), eggs and savory custard, barley, pasta, or potatoes. Although the flavor of ramps is subtle, it is worth singling out rather than burying it with a plethora of stronger ingredients.

PRESERVE

Ramp leaves can be chopped and dehydrated. The bulbs and leafstalks freeze well and are excellent pickled (using a pickled ramp in a martini instead of the usual onion is a forager's classic).

7

SHOOTS AND STALKS

WHETHER YOU'RE GATHERING the lemony, hollow-centered shoots of Japanese knotweed, the fat, cardoon-like immature flower stalks of burdock, or the just-starting-to-flower stalks of second-year garlic mustard plants, what you're looking for as far as the choicest edible parts is very much the same. The delectable part of both shoots and stalks is found in the growth area toward the tips, the part that is actively getting longer. In contrast, one of the main purposes of the bottom end of the shoot or stalk is simply to hold the rest of the plant upright. That part is usually too tough to be good eating.

I'm using the word "shoots" in this book to refer to the first spring growth of perennial plants including wild asparagus, Japanese knotweed, and pokeweed. These shoot straight up (pun intended) from the roots with few if any leaves unfurled, and look quite different—sometimes radically different—from the mature plants after they have had a few more months to grow.

By "stalks," I mean the flower stalks of annuals and biennials that may have already produced a full leaf rosette, but at a certain point in their development

Pokeweed shoots are one of the best wild treats of early spring, but must be harvested at the right stage and boiled to be edible. This unbranched, all-green (no pink stem) shoot is at the right stage for harvesting.

WARNING Unlike other edible wild shoots, pokeweed (*Phytolacca americana*) is toxic if harvested after the shoots begin to branch and/or turn reddish, and if they are not boiled before they are eaten.

send up prominent flower stalks. So rather than emerging directly from perennial roots, stems first, leaves later, these plants already have leaves (often in a rosette) and then shoot up stalks that will eventually be topped with flowers and then seeds. They will have edible leaves as well as shoots, and in some cases other edible parts as well. But often the stalk itself is the best vegetable on the plant. Garlic mustard, curly and broad-leaved dock, thistle, milk thistle, wild carrot, and salsify all produce delectable stalks.

To **harvest** only the yummy, tender part of most shoots and stalks, leaving the tough bases behind, use what I call the "bend-until-it-snaps" method. Start by gently trying to bend a shoot or stalk near the earth. It will likely bend but not snap. Work your way up toward the growth tip, 1 or 2 inches at a time, bending as you go. When you reach the divide between the supportive, fibrous base tissue and the tender, juicy growth tissue, it will snap where you tried to bend it (yes, exactly like bending cultivated asparagus spears until they snap at that divide point). Everything from the snap point to the growth tip is good eats.

Good ways to **prepare** wild edible shoots and stalks include steaming, stir-frying, boiling, or grilling, and many are also good raw. The exception is pokeweed, which *must* be boiled for food safety reasons.

Edible shoots and stalks **preserve** well by blanching and then freezing. Most (pokeweed excepted) may also be pickled with excellent results. Pressure canning shoots and stalks yields a mushy result—skip it.

Start by gently bending the shoot or stalk toward the bottom and working your way toward the tip.

PERENNIAL SHOOTS

Wild asparagus (*Asparagus*), Japanese knotweed (*Fallopia japonica* syn. *Polygonum cuspidatum*), milkweed (*Asclepias syriaca*), and pokeweed (*Phytolacca americana*) are four of my favorite wild foods that I look forward to each spring. A great way to find these edible shoots is to learn to identify the plants when they are in their full-grown stage in summer. At that point, they will look nothing like the shoots you want to eat next spring, but they will be very easy to identify. And because these perennials will come up in the exact same spot each year, you can make note of where you found them and start checking that place in spring.

WILD ASPARAGUS (*Asparagus* species)

FIND AND IDENTIFY

Wild asparagus will grow in anything from full sun to partial shade, but you're most likely to find it growing in edge environments. Look for it between the woods and the meadow, alongside country roads, or as a feral escape just outside the garden or farm fence.

In North America, the species you're most likely to find is *Asparagus officinalis*, which is the same as the cultivated asparagus. *A. aphyllus* is native to the Mediterranean and Middle East but has been introduced to some parts of Southern California. Asparagus is a perennial, meaning that it regrows from the same roots each year. *A. officinalis* dies back to the ground each winter, whereas *A. aphyllus* is evergreen.

A good way to get to know wild asparagus is to identify the mature plant in summer and then go back to the same place to harvest the spears the following spring. Or you could do a forager's cheat and learn to identify asparagus plants in a garden or on a farm and then be able to recognize it in the wild.

"Wait a minute," you may be thinking, "don't I already know what asparagus looks like?" For most people, the answer is a partial no: they know what the edible spears look like but not the mature plant. A mature asparagus plant looks as different from the shoot as a butterfly is from a caterpillar.

In early to mid-spring for *Asparagus officinalis*, or the winter rainy season for *A. aphyllus*, the familiar spears shoot up from the perennial roots. Like cultivated asparagus, they are topped with bracts that look like scales. Wild asparagus shoots tend to be skinnier than cultivated ones. Often the stalks are tinged with purple.

Those scale-like bracts eventually branch out. They become slender branches covered with feathery (or in the case of *Asparagus aphyllus*, spiky) feather foliage that is actually not leaves but thin green branches. Asparagus plants can grow as tall as 6 feet. The small, green, bell-shaped flowers grow in the leaf axils (where the leaves join the stems). Both male and female asparagus plants produce edible shoots, but the female plants produce red berries less than ½ inch in diameter that are poisonous.

HARVEST

The best technique for picking wild asparagus is the bend-until-it-snaps method described on page 88. Alternatively, slice off the shoots a couple of inches above the ground, then hold each shoot at either end and bend until it snaps to separate the tender, meristematic (active growth) part of the shoot from its tough base.

PREPARE

Anything you can do with cultivated asparagus, you can do with wild asparagus. The only difference is that it will taste much better. Wild asparagus usually has a slightly stronger asparagus taste, and an intriguing hint of both sweetness and bitterness. It is a more complex taste than tame asparagus, and utterly delicious. Aside from steaming, grilling, frying, and any other asparagus preparation you love, try eating some raw (arguably my favorite way to eat wild asparagus, although I don't like raw cultivated asparagus at all).

PRESERVE

Wild asparagus can be blanched and frozen, although you will lose some texture quality. A better option is to pickle it.

◄ Tall and feathery, mature asparagus plants look nothing like the familiar, edible shoots.

FLOWER STALKS

There is a moment in spring when many wild plants with edible leaves start to send up what will eventually become their flower stalks. Caught at the right time, these are some of the most delicious wild vegetables you can collect. The trick is to separate the tender from the tough parts of the stalks.

What you want to end up in your collection container is a mix of not-yet-bitter leaves, tender-crisp stems, and perhaps some immature flower bud clusters. Keep in mind that any already opened flower heads will be *much* more pungent than the rest of the plant (mustard flowers, for example: nice as a garnish but overpowering if you include too many). To collect at this broccoli rabe–like stage, start bending the stalks near the base and work your way up. At first the stalks will simply bend. But when you hit the spot where they snap cleanly and immediately, everything from that spot up is culinary gold.

Milk thistle (*Sylibum maritanum*) stalks are excellent raw or cooked once peeled.

TASTIEST EDIBLE FLOWER STALKS

Tasty edible flower stalks include burdock, mustard, garlic mustard, curly dock, broad-leaved dock, and milk thistle.

GARLIC MUSTARD (*Alliaria petiolata*)

Many gardeners swear disapprovingly if you mention this plant because it is so invasive, yet garlic mustard is a fantastic wild food with a spicy, pungent flavor that hints at horseradish. Several parts of the plant are edible (including the roots, leaves, flowers, and seeds), but the best by far comes into season when it starts to send up flower stalks in its second calendrical year.

FIND AND IDENTIFY

Unlike many other invasive species that prefer to grow in full, direct sunlight, garlic mustard thrives in partial sunlight or even partial shade. It does like quite a bit of sunlight early in the year, which is why it often grows under deciduous trees (the garlic mustard gets a jump-start dose of sunlight while the tree's branches are still bare in early spring).

This is garlic mustard at its most delicious "broccoli rabe" stage when it has just begun to flower.

Garlic mustard is a biennial, growing a rosette of heart- or kidney-shaped leaves the first year, overwintering, and then flowering and going to seed the following year. The leaves have rounded teeth on the margins and a net-like pattern of veins.

As spring warms up and the trees start to leaf out, garlic mustard sends up flower stalks that can grow to be 2½ feet tall. At first, the flowers look like miniature broccoli heads; eventually each bud in the flower head opens into a tiny, four-petaled white flower. The alternately arranged leaves on the flower stalk are more triangular than the basal leaves. The slender seed capsules are 1 to 2½ inches long. They start out green and tender, and eventually become straw colored. Each seed capsule has two rows of black or very dark brown seeds separated by a papery membrane.

An important part of identifying garlic mustard is to use your nose. All parts of the plant, when crushed, do indeed have a garlicky-mustardy scent.

HARVEST

Sustainability is not an issue with garlic mustard: not only does it spread prolifically by seed, but it has allelopathic roots (they exude chemicals that can eventually discourage other plants from growing next to it). The only caution with harvesting garlic mustard is that if you are collecting the seeds you want to take as much care as possible not to accidentally spread them around.

The first-year rosette leaves are slightly bitter, but not terribly so, and are available almost year-round even in cold winter areas. Simply twist off entire clusters of leaf rosettes to harvest. By far the tastiest stage to harvest is in the second year when the plants send up flower stalks. Use the bend-until-it-snaps method to harvest the stalks, along with any leaves on them. If your stalks also have a few flower heads with mostly unopened buds (a few of the little white flowers is okay), so much the better. While still green, the seedpods are a tasty raw nibble. They are easy to strip off the (by then) tough stalks.

By mid-summer, the plants start to die off, and the seedpods turn dry and cream to tan colored. Harvest and clean the seeds within using the general harvesting and winnowing methods on page 151. If it's the roots you're after, look for garlic mustard plants that have no flower stalks yet, only the basal rosette of leaves. Once the plant starts to flower, the roots will be too tough to bother with.

PREPARE

Leaves from the basal rosettes of first-year and early second-year garlic mustard have a slight bitter edge but are still good mixed with other cool-weather greens such as chickweed. They are good in pesto, a classic among foragers.

Once the flower stalks start to shoot up, the plant resembles broccoli rabe in both flavor and appearance, and is good in any recipe that calls for that vegetable. Although garlic mustard roots never get as stout and substantial as horseradish roots, they have a similar flavor. Minced fine and combined with vinegar or mayonnaise, they are an excellent condiment.

Add green, immature garlic mustard seedpods to pickles, stir-fries, kimchi, and anywhere else a spicy kick is welcome. Use the fully mature seeds as you would whole mustard seeds in pickle spice blends or curries, or grind them to make your own prepared mustard.

PRESERVE

The best way to preserve garlic mustard stalks, leaves, and immature flower heads is to blanch and freeze them (or chop, sauté in a little oil, and then freeze). The dried seeds can be stored for at least six months.

RULE BREAKER

BURDOCK (*Arctium* species)

The stalks of second-year burdock plants before they flower are my favorite part of the plant to eat. The roots are good, the leafstalks passable, but when cooked the immature flower stalks have a wonderful texture, like artichoke hearts or cardoons, and a delightful mild flavor. What makes burdock a rule breaker? Often the best stalks are as thick as an inch across and too sturdy to gather with the bend-until-it-snaps method. Also, unlike many other edible stalks, once peeled they are good to eat almost all the way down to the base.

FIND AND IDENTIFY

Burdock grows in sun or partial sunlight. It is a biennial that grows a rosette of leaves in its first year of growth, then flowers and goes to seed the following

Although burdock's taproot is the better-known food this plant produces, for my money the immature flower stalks are a much tastier vegetable. They are also much easier to harvest!

calendar year. It loves disturbed soils and is a common weed of farms, gardens, and parks.

The leaves can be huge, up to 2 feet long and 1 foot wide. They remind some people of rhubarb plants, but unlike rhubarb's leaves, burdock leaves have a felt-y, fuzzy texture and are whitish on the undersides (and unlike rhubarb leaves, burdock leaves are not poisonous). Although untoothed, the margins of the leaves are wavy, almost ruffled. A burdock root is shaped like a slender carrot but brown on the outside and a lighter color within.

In the spring of its second calendar year, after overwintering, burdock sends up a stalk that will eventually bear brush-like purplish flowers. These are followed by the burrs from which the plant gets its common name. Burdock burrs are what inspired George de Mestral to invent and patent Velcro.

HARVEST
Look for the flower stalks shooting up from the center of the leaf rosettes. Choose ones that are nice and fat but that are still unbranched and have not yet begun to produce flower buds: usually these will be between 8 and 18 inches tall. Although the bend-until-it-snaps method is perfect for most shoots and stalks, burdock's flower stalks are so sturdy that you will usually need to use a knife to slice across the stalk close to where it emerges from the basal leaves.

The roots of first-year burdock plants are a good vegetable that is known as *gobo* in Japan. How do you know you've got a first-year plant? It won't have any flower stalks, only a leaf rosette. The roots are also used in herbal medicine for chronic skin, digestive system, and liver ailments.

PREPARE
With a sharp paring knife, peel the fibrous outer layer off the stalks. As with artichoke hearts, delicious cores will start to discolor soon after being exposed to air. If this bothers you, have a bowl of acidulated water (about a gallon of water with 1 to 2 tablespoons of vinegar or lemon juice added, or ½ teaspoon of citric acid) ready to put the peeled stalks into until you are ready to cook them. Burdock stalks are wonderful steamed, boiled, or baked into casseroles.

PRESERVE
Peeled burdock stalks can be blanched and then frozen. To use, simply put the frozen burdock stalks (no need to thaw first) in water, bring to a boil, then reduce heat and simmer until almost tender. Finish cooking them in soups, stir-fries, or casseroles.

8

FLOWERS, POLLEN, AND BUDS

FLOWERS, POLLEN, AND BUDS might seem like minor players in a forager's annual food haul, but they deserve to be featured. To get an idea of the culinary potential of edible flowers, just imagine sipping some dandelion flower wine along with a creamy sauté of buttered milkweed buds served inside a cattail pollen crepe.

Wisteria's beautiful flowers are edible and deliciously perfumed, but all other parts of this woody vine are poisonous.

FLOWERS

Colorful, fragrant, and often surprisingly packed with flavor, I think edible flowers are frequently overlooked as a wild food because we are not used to buying them at the supermarket. At best, most people are only familiar with them as a pretty salad garnish. But edible flowers can be much more than decoration. Let's talk about pickled redbud blossoms that look delicately pink but taste like lemony green beans or hauntingly perfumed wisteria blossom wine. How about trying magenta-colored dried bee balm blooms on your pizza instead of similar tasting oregano? Or yellow mustard flowers that are even spicier than the rest of the plant? Clover "flour" in your muffins? Dandelion fritters? Elderflower "champagne"?

> **WARNING** Just because a plant has edible flowers does *not* mean all its other parts are safe to eat as well. Examples of plants with edible flowers but poisonous leaves, stems, and/or roots include elderberry, honeysuckle, violet, and wisteria.

As versatile and tasty as wild edible flowers are, a few important precautions apply when harvesting. As a rule, if you can eat the fruit, you can also eat the flower and the unopened flower bud. This means that wild trees and shrubs that produce edible fruits—including hawthorn, pears, black cherries, and crabapples—all have edible buds and flowers. However, this does *not* mean that other parts of the plant are edible.

Because all fruits come from flowers, each flower you **harvest** means there will be one less fruit. But since you are unlikely to be able to pick all the flowers on a tall fruit tree or shrub even if you try, plenty of fruit will almost certainly remain for both you and wildlife. Nonetheless, it is conceivable that you could remove all the flower heads from a small elderberry shrub, resulting in no fruit on that plant this year. It is smarter to graze, taking just a few flower heads from one plant and then moving on to another plant.

Many flowers are fragile and decline rapidly once plucked from their parent plant. Chicory, for example, rarely makes it home in good shape if it takes you more than 30 minutes to get it on the table. And I've put dandelion flowers in a plastic bag in the freezer only to find a week later that all I've got is a bag of white seed fluff and shriveled calyxes: the flowers went to seed even after I froze them. Other flowers such as redbud, black locust, wisteria, and violet flowers are a bit sturdier and will keep in covered containers in the fridge for at least a week. With any edible flower, a good technique is to wrap them in a damp but not dripping wet cloth or paper towel until you can get them home.

All edible flowers are excellent raw and make colorful salad garnishes. They can also be **prepared** as colorful syrups that can then be turned into awesome drinks and desserts. Not all edible flowers refrigerate or freeze well. The ones that do tend to be irregular (non-symmetrical) with somewhat fleshy petals such as redbud, violet, and black locust. Symmetrical flowers with thin petals or ray flowers such as dandelion and chicory don't hold up as well. All edible flowers can be used to add flavor and color to jellies, homemade wines, vinegars, and herbal teas. Sturdier edible flowers such as redbud can also be pickled.

Hawthorn (*Crataegus*) species flowers are edible as is the fruit, but the aroma disagrees with some people.

All edible flowers can be **preserved** by packing them in sugar or honey (honeysuckle sugar makes a fantastic glass-rimmer for cocktails), or infusing them in wine or other alcohol. Or you can go the longer alcoholic route (your patience will be rewarded!), and ferment your own flower wine (you may need to add yeast—wild or otherwise—and sugar; see the resources). You can preserve most flowers, including violets, redbud, wisteria, and black locust, by candying them. To do so, dip them in some beaten egg white and then coat with granulated sugar. Let dry on waxed paper and use to garnish cakes and desserts. Dried edible flowers are as versatile as fresh for uses ranging from soup (daylily petals) to seasoning (oregano-like bee balm) to herbal tea (basswood, goldenrod).

BLACK LOCUST (*Robinia pseudoacacia*)

FIND AND IDENTIFY

Native to eastern North America, black locust trees have been introduced to several continents and are considered invasive in some regions. Look for them near humans: landscapers love their gorgeous flowers, attractive foliage, and drought and pollution tolerance, so they are frequently planted in parks, as street trees, and in gardens. But because of their invasive nature, they often "jump the fence" and can be found growing wild just outside such locations. They also spread by suckers that pop up from the roots.

Growing up to 80 feet tall, black locust trees have thick, deeply furrowed brown-gray bark. Like other members of the legume family (Fabaceae), black locust has compound leaves and irregular flowers (the petals are not all the same size and shape). Each leaf will have between three and eleven leaflets, which are oval with smooth edges. The fragrant stemmed flowers (usually creamy off-white; sometimes pink and pale green) grow in thick hanging clusters.

HARVEST

Look for black locust flowers in spring, usually just after wisteria bloom time has ended. Snip off the whole flower clusters using scissors or pruners. For the best texture, gather only recently unfurled flower clusters that are plump and fragrant. You are not harming the tree by harvesting the flowers, and in fact may be doing an environmental good deed by preventing this often-invasive species from producing seeds. Both the pods and the seeds within are sweetest once the pods have turned brown. Black locust flowers will keep for several days in the fridge. If you are unable to get them into a refrigerator within an hour of collecting, place them in a moist cloth bag or roll them in a dampened dish towel.

PREPARE

Black locust flowers are wonderful in any recipe that captures their fragrance. Try them raw in salads and spring rolls, make them into jelly or wine, or experiment with black locust fritters—a classic wild food preparation. The pods can be simply chewed on (children love this wild "candy"), or use the preparation method in chapter 10 to make black locust pod powder. The seeds can be boiled until tender and eaten.

As flavorful as they are beautiful, black locust flowers bring an exotic perfumed essence to recipes ranging from desserts to fritters to wine.

WARNING Only the flowers, pods, and seeds of *Robinia pseudoacacia* are edible. All other parts of the tree are toxic.

PRESERVE

Black locust flowers freeze well. Once defrosted, use the flowers for fritters, jelly, or other uses where the taste matters more than the texture. You can lacto-ferment black locust flowers into an interesting relish, or preserve them in an alcohol base (fermented into wine or infused into a base such as vodka).

Non-Aromatic Edible Flowers

Flowers that do not have a strong fragrance or taste can still contribute color, texture, and nutrition to a recipe. Dandelion (*Taraxacum officinale*), common blue violet (*Viola sororia*), all the clovers (*Trifolium*), chicory (*Cichorium intybus*), and many others are in this category.

As with all edible flowers, it's best to **harvest** by pinching them off when they have just opened but before they have started to lose their color or go to seed. Try to eat or prepare/preserve these as soon as possible. They do not hold up well if stored, even in the refrigerator. But if you're in the field and absolutely must hold them over for a couple of hours, use the Damp Bag Method on page 14.

Non-aromatic edible flowers are terrific as salad garnishes, but they really come into their own when used in omelets, fritters, grain-based salads, and stir-fries. And then there's arguably my favorite **preparation** for these types of

Better known for its edible roots and leaves, chicory's beautiful blue flowers make a lovely salad garnish.

edible flowers: flower flour. Many neutrally flavored flowers including clover and dandelion (petals only; no bitter green calyxes) can be dried and crushed into an ingredient that really has no commercial counterpart. I'm calling these dried and ground or crushed flowers "flour" because they can be used in wheat flour–based recipes such as bread, pancakes, dumplings, and muffins. Keep in mind, though, that the recipe will fall apart if you use 100 percent flower flour. A good ratio is usually 25 percent flower to 75 percent traditional flour.

Dried, these non-aromatic flowers add color, nutrition, and texture to recipes but not any noticeable flavor. To keep their colorful contribution, **preserve** them by drying them in a dehydrator on the lowest heat setting or air dry. Store them away from direct light or heat in storage. You can make jelly and wine from non-aromatic flowers. They don't freeze particularly well.

RED CLOVER (*Trifolium pratense*)

FIND AND IDENTIFY
Like other clovers (plants in the *Trifolium* genus), red clover likes disturbed soil and full to partial sun. That kind of habitat is exactly what we humans create in our gardens, roadsides, and parks, and those are exactly the places you are most likely to find clover. Like other plants in the legume family (Fabaceae), clover has the super power of being able to fix atmospheric nitrogen into the soil, replenishing earth that intensive farming has depleted. For that reason, organic farmers frequently plant it as a cover crop, and it's not unusual to find it growing as an escape plant just outside the farm.

Red clover grows to about 16 inches tall, but the plants can be a bit floppy and therefore look shorter. It has three leaflets per leaf, and each leaflet may have an off-white chevron mark. Both the leaves and the stalks are somewhat hairy. The flower heads are made up of many pink to pink-purple florets grouped in globe-shaped pom-poms ½ to 1¼ inches in diameter.

HARVEST
Peak red clover flowering time is mid-spring through early summer, depending on where you live. After that, it may bloom sporadically but not enough to make

Flower "flour" is my favorite way to use red clover. Also good as a beverage and raw in salads, when dried clover's surprisingly sturdy flowers add sponginess and gentle sweetness to breads, pancakes, muffins, etc.

harvesting efficient. An exception is places where the plants get mowed: in that situation, the plants may flower more prolifically over a longer amount of time.

A couple of leaves are usually nestled close to the base of the flower head. Don't worry about avoiding these when you are harvesting the flowers (it would be too labor intensive to try to do so). They are also edible, and neutral as far as flavor and texture. You are not harming this short-lived but perennial plant by collecting its flower heads and upper leaves. And in any case, it is considered an invasive in some regions.

Red clover has been shown to be useful for treating skin diseases, breast cancer, and respiratory ailments. And it can replenish the nitrogen in intensively farmed soil. Whew! Super hero.

PREPARE

The florets of red clover flowers and other clovers (they are all edible) are usually attached to a tough core. That's not a problem if you are making an herbal infusion since you'll strain them out anyway. But if using the raw flowers in salads or grain dishes, it's best to strip them off that tough core.

Dried red clover florets, stripped of that core and ground, add a lovely texture and color to baked goods, spoonbreads, and pancakes. Pulse-dry red clover flower heads in a food processor to quickly separate the florets. After that, feel through with your clean hands to find and remove any tough cores. You can replace up to 25 percent of the traditional flour in any baked good recipe with dried red clover flour.

PRESERVE

Drying is the best way to preserve red clover flowers. A dehydrator works (use the lowest heat setting). Or place them in a thin layer (not more than 1 inch thick) in a cloth or paper bag and turn the bag over daily to promote good air circulation. What does *not* work is exposing the clover flower heads to heat or light. Instead of turning from pink to purple, they turn brown and lose all of their visual appeal in recipes as well as developing an "off" taste.

Strongly Aromatic Flowers

Honeysuckle (*Lonicera*), lilac (*Syringa*), some roses (*Rosa*), basswood (*Tilia*), and a few other edible flowers are so strongly perfumed that they are better used as a flavoring than as the main bulk of a recipe.

Although the basic method is the same as for other edible flowers, getting aromatic flowers quickly from **harvest** to preparation or preservation is especially important. The same volatile essential oils that give them their scent also give them their flavor, and those oils do not last long once the flower is severed from the plant.

Raw (and recently harvested) strongly aromatic flowers are wonderful as a garnish, but choose neutral background flavors such as a mild cheese, green salad, or rice as their flavor tends to overwhelm anything else in the dish. All edible aromatic flowers are good **prepared** as tea, especially "sun tea." For that, put the raw flowers into a pitcher of cold water and cover tightly. Leave in the sun for an hour or two, strain, sweeten to taste, chill, and serve.

Despite having fewer petals than more ornamental horticultural roses, roses with a single ring of petals are often much more intensely aromatic and flavorful.

Fragrant flowers are among the best wild ingredients for alcoholic beverages. You can **preserve** their essence by infusing them in syrup, vodka, or brandy, and then use those in cocktails and desserts. You can also make interesting aperitif wines by infusing aromatic edible flowers in semi-dry white wine overnight.

Another way to preserve such flowers is to put a ½-inch layer of granulated sugar in a container, sprinkle over a layer of fresh flowers, then repeat layers of sugar and flowers until you've used up your harvest, finishing with a layer of sugar on top. Cover and set aside for 3 days. Tap the sugar through a sieve to strain out the flowers. Store the now-perfumed sugar in tightly sealed containers away from direct light or heat, and use it in desserts including homemade ice cream, or in hot or cold drinks.

HONEYSUCKLE (*Lonicera* species)

FIND AND IDENTIFY

Honeysuckles are drooping (if unpruned) shrubs or twining vines with untoothed, rounded leaves that join the stems in pairs (opposite leaf arrangement). They grow in a range of light conditions from full sun to partial shade.

The fragrant flowers are tubular. In the most widespread species, the flowers start out off-white, becoming a creamy yellow as they age. The fruits are round berries with several seeds and red, purple, or black depending on species. Although some species have edible fruit, the berries of most honeysuckles are toxic.

When I was a child, I learned to sip the sweet drop of nectar at the base of honeysuckle flowers. It turns out that is not the only way to enjoy them.

HARVEST

Several *Lonicera* species are considered invasive, and in any case you are not endangering the plant by harvesting the flowers. Therefore, sustainability is not an issue with honeysuckle flowers. To harvest, pinch off individual honeysuckle flowers and rush them to the salt, sugar, syrup, alcohol, or another medium that is waiting to extract their aroma and flavor.

PREPARE

My first and favorite way to eat honeysuckle flowers is the one I learned as a child. It hardly counts as a preparation method: simply pluck a honeysuckle flower from the vine and suck on the stem end. The drop of nectar you'll be rewarded with is tiny but delicious. Raw honeysuckle flowers make a terrific garnish for cakes and other desserts. You can also infuse them in gently heated cream and then use that to make a wonderful ice cream.

PRESERVE

Honeysuckle readily imparts its flavor and aroma to sugar or alcohol. Note that it does not dry or freeze well. Honeysuckle honey, made by simply infusing honeysuckle flowers in a light, mild-flavored honey, transforms iced tea into something extraordinary.

POLLEN

Pollen is rich in nutrients including protein, and can be a very versatile and tasty ingredient. Some pollens such as cattail and pine pollen are useful as flour in pancakes, pasta, fritters, and baked goods. Others such as fennel pollen are intensely flavored and best to use in tiny amounts as seasonings rather than main ingredients. Note that the harvesting, preparing, and preserving methods for mild flour-like pollen and intensely flavored seasoning pollen are basically the same. During all your handling of wild edible pollen from harvest to cooking, keep in mind that the lightest breeze through your kitchen window or a sneeze could send your featherlight harvest flying.

The key to **harvesting** pollen is to capture it *before* you snip off the pollen-bearing part of the plant. This means putting a bag over the flower head first, and then using scissors or pruners to snip it into the bag. Over the next day

SOME OF MY FAVORITE EDIBLE FLOWERS

This is not even close to a complete list of all the edible flowers out there. I've limited it to edible flowers that grow either wild or feral. Remember that just because a flower is edible doesn't mean the rest of the plant is safe to eat. Elderberry, for example, has edible flowers and fruit, but the rest of the plant is poisonous.

Anise Hyssop
Apple
Asiatic Dayflower
Basswood (Linden)
Black Locust
Cherry
Chicory
Crabapple
Clover
Dandelion
Daylily
Elderberry

Evening Primrose
Fennel
Garlic Mustard
Goldenrod
Honeysuckle
Magnolia
Mallow
Milkweed
Monarda
Mustard
Oxeye Daisy
Pear

Pineappleweed
Plum
Redbud
Rose
Sow Thistle
Violet
Wild Carrot
Wisteria
Wood Sorrel
Yucca

Yucca blossoms are excellent slow-cooked (roasted, stir-fried over low heat, etc.) and good in both savory and sweet recipes.

WARNING People with severe seasonal allergies, as well as pregnant women, should avoid eating pollen.

or two, the pollen will drop from the collected plant matter into the bag. Use paper bags or tightly woven cloth bags (I use sturdy muslin produce bags). The pollen needs some air so it doesn't start to mold, but it could slip through thin or loosely woven cloth bags.

Humans are not the only foragers who collect pollen, so it's common to find a few insects mixed in with your pollen harvest (especially with cattail pollen). My answer to this is (1) freeze the freshly harvested pollen (this kills the insects), and (2) shake the pollen through a fine-mesh sieve into a bowl. The insects will be left behind in the sieve.

Once your pollen is thus **prepared**, you can use it immediately, freeze it for future use, or dry it out before storing in airtight containers. Use mildly flavored pollens as an addition to grain flours in any recipe. I do not recommend using only pollen in baked or fried recipes: the texture will not be good. But the color and flavor of pollen-enriched food can be spectacular—c'mon over for some sunshine-colored cattail pollen pancakes. Use strongly aromatic pollen (wild fennel, some pines) as a spice.

Preserve pollen for several months by storing in airtight containers away from direct light or heat. Be certain the pollen is fully dry before sealing it in the container or it will mold. For longer storage, the freezer is the best option.

◀ Cattail's male flowers grow stacked on the female flowers, and give foragers abundant amounts of pollen that makes a delicious golden-colored flour.

WILD FENNEL (*Foeniculum vulgare*)

FIND AND IDENTIFY

Wild fennel grows abundantly in much of North and South America, the United Kingdom, South Africa, India, and Australia, as well as around its native habitat in countries that border the Mediterranean. Fennel loves full sun. It is drought tolerant and therefore often found in dry, rocky soils. Where it is abundant, it is most frequently found along roadsides. It is considered an invasive species throughout its range, and sustainability is not an issue when harvesting wild fennel.

The plants grow from 4 to 9 feet tall (unless they have been nibbled shorter by the deer and other wildlife that eat this food). It is common to find both last year's dead stalks and the new green and juicy ones of this perennial on the same plant.

Fennel leaves are feathery and look very much like dill. The bases of the leafstalks usually clasp the main upright stems, which are branched, hollow, and as thick as ¾-inch diameter. The mustard-yellow flowers grow in umbels 2 to 4 inches across and are in season for several months from spring through early summer. This is your window of time for the pollen harvest.

The seeds look exactly like their commercially sold kin. They are small (3–8.5 mm by 2–2.5 mm), football-shaped, ribbed, and green to yellow-brown depending on when you find them. The seeds have been used medicinally for thousands of years for purposes ranging from digestive aid to galactagogue (increases milk in nursing mothers). An interesting medicinal use is a cooled and strained decoction of the seeds as an eyewash to reduce redness and irritation, sort of a natural Visine.

Every part of wild fennel has a strong anise smell when crushed, and this should be an important part of how you identify this plant.

HARVEST

Use the general harvesting method described on page 110 to collect the pollen. Look for bright yellow flower umbels with most of the florets already opened. Although I only get a tiny bit of pollen (about ⅛ teaspoon from each flower umbel), I don't mind because I'll be using this as a spice, not a flour. The harvest quantity may be tiny, but the flavor is huge. Harvest the leaves and stalks by cutting them off the plants with a knife, scissors, or pruners. The easiest way to gather the seeds is to snip off whole seed umbels.

Wild fennel never produces a rounded bulb like the vegetable you buy at markets. But there are many other delicious ingredients you can get from this plant including the leaves, stalks, flowers, and seeds. And the pollen is one of the finest spices you'll ever taste.

PREPARE

Use wild fennel pollen as a seasoning. Its anise-y aroma is strong but at the same time subtler than the seeds or leaves. The pollen is heavenly on roasted root vegetables, or dusted over a mild goat cheese. But it can also go in a sweet direction in cookies, custards, and other desserts. You can use whole fennel flower heads to flavor pickles (bonus: they look pretty in the jars). Fennel leaves are traditionally used fresh in salads, soups, and seafood dishes; they are also a fun switch-out for dill in pickle recipes. The seeds can be used in both sweet and savory dishes. They are a common ingredient in many curry blends.

PRESERVE

Freeze fennel stalks to add to soup stocks—they are strongly flavored but go well with fish—or candy them. The seeds, flower heads, and pollen dry well and make excellent seasonings. Although they each have that characteristic licorice flavor, they also each have distinctly different tastes. It's best to use fennel leaves fresh as they do not dry or freeze well.

BUDS

The unopened flowers that we call buds can be fabulous food. Ever eat broccoli or cauliflower? Those are both clusters of immature flower buds. Wild flower buds including those of sow thistle (*Sonchus oleraceus*), daylily (*Hemerocallis fulva*), milkweed (*Asclepias syriaca*), magnolia (*Magnolia*), and garlic mustard (*Alliaria petiolata*) are all wonderful foods.

Flower buds are all about timing: for most culinary uses you want to **harvest** them still tightly closed, with no hint of the eventual flower color showing. When and where this happens varies from region to region, but spring is *the* season for buds pretty much everywhere. Most buds, and clusters of buds, can be easily pinched off the plant without any tools other than your hands. Although you are not harming the plant by harvesting the immature flower buds, you are reducing the amount of seeds the plant will produce. And, in some cases (elderberry, crabapple, cherry, viburnum, for example), the amount of edible fruit you might enjoy later in the season. Also remember that you are not the only animal eating from these plants: In the case of trees and tall shrubs, that's usually not a problem because the flowers (and eventually fruits) that are out of reach will be dinner for wildlife. But in the case of

Well after sow thistle's leaves have become too bitter to bother with, the unopened flower buds are ready to harvest.

low-growing plants such as milkweed (a primary food for the monarch butter-fly), harvest sparingly unless you are in a meadow with an abundance of the species you want to harvest (and even then, notice how much you are leaving behind and be glad that you did).

Prepare mild-flavored unopened edible flower buds, including those of gar-lic mustard and milkweed, by pickling, steaming, stir-frying, or adding them to pretty much any recipe where broccoli would work. Smaller buds such as those of sow thistle and wild lettuce are better pickled.

Besides **preserving** edible flower buds via lacto-fermentation or vinegar-based pickling methods, you can briefly (1 minute) blanch and then freeze. They can also be pressure canned for long-term storage at room temperature. Buds are not good candidates for dehydration.

MILKWEED (*Asclepias syriaca*)

FIND AND IDENTIFY
Milkweed is a North American native that prefers sunny fields but will also show up alongside partially shaded paths. Although numerous species are called "milkweed," here I am only describing *Asclepias syriaca*, the milkweed that brings a sparkle to any forager's eye.

Milkweed plants shoot up on unbranching stalks, a very important charac-teristic that distinguishes them from poisonous look-similar dogbane (I gen-erally avoid anything with the word "bane" in its common name)—but note that in early spring this can be tricky because both dogbane and milkweed start their growth unbranched. Milkweed, however, doesn't branch even when mature. And dogbane is hairless, whereas milkweed wears a fine fuzz.

In spring, look for slim, unbranched shoots that have a few oval, fuzzy leaves with smooth margins at the tips. Snap off a piece of any part of a milkweed plant and it will ooze the white latex that gives the plant its common name. Alas, dogbane also oozes latex, so that alone does not clinch your ID.

Mature milkweed plants can grow 3 to 6 feet tall, still only rarely (almost never) branching. The leaves attach to the stems in pairs (an opposite leaf arrangement) and are 3 to 9 inches long and half as wide, with an oblong shape and untoothed edges. The flower heads when young and green look like minia-ture broccoli. As they mature in the leaf axils of the top 1 or 2 feet of the plants,

Milkweed bud clusters look a bit like miniature broccoli and are one of the best wild vegetables.

Once fully opened, milkweed flowers can be used to flavor and beautifully color cordials and syrups.

Young milkweed pods look somewhat like mutant okra and are delicious cooked.

they open into more loosely clustered, round, pink to purple rounded flower heads with numerous small flowers. Each tiny flower has five parts that bend downward like a skirt, as well as five that stand upright with the central parts of the flower.

Milkweed seedpods are unlike most every other plant part you'll encounter in summer. Imagine sharply curved okra pods, pointed on one end, with bumps on their surfaces. They are 2 to 5 inches long. When mature, they are squishy and filled with white fluff.

Other milkweeds are similar looking especially at the spring shoot stage. However, they are bitter and *Asclepias syriaca* is not. It is safe to take a tiny nibble and spit it out. If it is bitter, you've got the wrong plant.

HARVEST

Milkweed is one of the only foods of the monarch butterfly caterpillar. Harvest by gleaning a shoot here, a floret there, a pod from this plant and then another plant. By grazing you will be leaving plenty behind for other species.

The mid- to late-spring shoots are the trickiest milkweed ingredient to distinguish from poisonous dogbane. If you're unsure, wait for the flower heads and pods, which are unmistakable. But if you're sure you've got *Asclepias syr-iaca* shoots, harvest them while they are still tender enough to snap off easily. Use scissors, pruners, or a small knife to harvest the still-green flower heads (my favorite milkweed part) as well as the pink-purple mature flowers. Use the same tools (or your hand) to harvest the immature seedpods, but give the pods a squeeze first. They should be quite firm rather than squishy. They will be less than 1 inch, or not much longer, at this optimal harvest stage. Be prepared for your blade and/or fingers to be covered in white latex.

PREPARE

Milkweed is a beautiful native plant that gives us four different foods—shoots, flowers, pods, and immature seed fluff. The tender-enough-to-snap-off shoots are great steamed, boiled, or stir-fried. The still-green flower heads can be prepared just like the shoots as well as pickled. The fully open flowers are aromatic and colorful and make great cordial and jelly. The immature, still-firm and green pods are best boiled or stir-fried. Inside the immature pods is a white substance that will eventually become the dry, fluffy seeds. Caught at the right stage, this is a unique wild foods ingredient that when cooked does a good job of mimicking the texture of semi-melted cheese. Use only the white, still-moist insides of the pods for this use, rejecting any that have begun to turn into seed fluff.

If you read foraging advice that dates from the early to mid-twentieth century, you'll likely be told that milkweed needs to be boiled in multiple changes of water to render it nontoxic. Not true. However, a small percentage of people are allergic to milkweed and will get violent tummy upset if they eat any part of the plant. As with any new-to-you food, wild or otherwise, always begin with just a taste and wait a while to see whether it agrees with your digestive system as much as your taste buds before digging in to a bowlful.

PRESERVE

The green, immature flower heads, shoots, and young seedpods can be blanched or stir-fried and then frozen. They may also be canned, or blanched and then pickled. The flavor and color of the mature flowers can be infused in alcohol or syrup.

RULE BREAKER

MAGNOLIA (*Magnolia* species)

FIND AND IDENTIFY

Widely planted by landscapers for their showy spring flowers, which can be as big as 3 inches across, magnolias cause grumpiness in property owners who have to sweep up the copious fallen petals. And after that fabulous spring show, the plant is nondescript and useless for the rest of the year, right? Wrong!

All magnolia trees and shrubs have large, oval, leathery, untoothed leaves. The leaves grow alternately on the branches but may appear whorled near the branch tips. They are usually unlobed but a few species may be lobed in a heart shape at the base. The leaf scars on the branches of this deciduous tree are prominent. The twigs are aromatic when scratched.

The famous flowers bloom in early spring in colors ranging from white to pale pink to deep magenta. The petals can be rounded or strap-like depending on the species and are arranged spirally. The fruits are cone-like and unusual among deciduous hardwood trees, with scales that are also in a spiral pattern.

The part we're interested in as an intriguing wild seasoning is the bud, which is shaped like a pointed bullet and is extremely fuzzy. Magnolias produce flower buds during the summer after they finish their spring blossoming. That means the buds you see on the trees that persist through the winter are next spring's floral display waiting to happen. They are also tasty.

HARVEST

Gather tightly closed, fuzzy magnolias buds anytime from summer through winter. It's easy to twist them off the stems. Remember that every bud you harvest is one less blossom for spring's show. For that reason, I usually harvest only the buds on the inside of the tree closest to the trunk, leaving the buds on the outer branches to become the flowers that everyone is looking forward to.

PREPARE

Use fresh or dried magnolia buds as a seasoning by grating them into recipes, or by lightly crushing and then infusing them. For example, you can infuse magnolia buds in gently heated milk before making a custard, or steep them in an alcohol base such as vodka for cocktails.

Magnolia buds can be harvested from late summer straight through until early spring of the following year.

PRESERVE

Preserve magnolia buds by covering them with a neutrally flavored alcohol (I recommend vodka), simmering them in a simple sugar syrup for 30 minutes and then straining them out or by drying them. If you opt for the latter, simply dry them in a paper or cloth bag: do not use heat (even the lowest heat setting of a dehydrator) and do not expose them to light. Store dried magnolia buds whole, and grate to use as needed (they will lose most of their aroma quickly if ground before storing).

◄ Neither a main course ingredient like milkweed or garlic mustard florets, nor a pickled caper substitute candidate like sow thistle buds, magnolia buds are an aromatic spice with an intriguing mix of clove, rose, and camphor.

9

FRUIT

FRUIT IS A GIFT FROM THE SUNNIEST MONTHS of the year. From the first strawberries to juicy beach plums to the tangy crabapples of autumn, these are some of the most sought-after wild foods. Botanically speaking, a fruit is "the seed-bearing part of the plant." By that scientifically correct definition, many of the foods we call "vegetables" are actually fruits. Cucumbers are fruits, for example, and so are green beans, and, well, any other plant part that has seeds.

Elderberries ripen in late summer. Unlike other fruits that are at their best raw, elderberries benefit from being dried or turned into jelly, wine, balsamic sauce, and other preparations.

The ways we usually use the words "fruit" and "vegetable" are a cook's distinction, not a botanist's. For this section, I am using the cook's distinction.

Experienced foragers and botanists, bear with me here, but there is a point I have to make because it is one I encounter so very often in my foraging classes. Many people nowadays are so far removed from plants and the true sources of their nourishment that they don't know that all fruits come from flowers. So yes, if you pick a cherry blossom to garnish your salad, there will be one less cherry on that tree later in the year. I'm not saying not to pick the occasional blossom, but as with all harvesting, be aware of the consequences. And be aware that when the flowers fall from a tree or shrub or patch of canes, that's your signal to start watching for the fruit.

WARNING Just because the fruit is edible does not necessarily mean that the rest of the plant is edible. Elderberries, for example, have edible fruits and flowers, but the rest of the shrub is poisonous.

When you **harvest** the fruit of a plant you do not harm the plant. Other animals than human do eat fruits, but it is extremely unlikely that you would so deplete the fruit supply as to endanger their food supply. For example, you probably won't make it all the way to the back of that thorny blackberry patch, and there's no way you're getting all the fruit at the top of that 40-foot wild black cherry tree.

The wild fruits of late spring and summer, such as berries and plums, tend to be juicy and easy to crush. These are best gathered in hard-sided containers rather than bags, and not piled so deeply that the fruit on the bottom gets crushed by the fruit on the top. The harder fruits of late summer and autumn, such as apples, pears, and hawthorn, are fine in bags or containers, but of course don't bang them around so hard that they get bruised.

When gathering windfall fruit—meaning fruit that has already fallen from the plant to the ground, be alert to signs that grubs, worms, and other creepy crawlies got to this food before you did. Telltale signs are small holes or dark spots on the outside of the fruit.

Prickly pear requires a special approach because of the glochids, tiny prickers that are annoyingly painful if they get into your skin. My preferred way of harvesting them painlessly is to use a cutoff plastic bottle for protection when twisting off the fruits.

Most but not all wild fruits are as good raw and without seasoning as **prepared** in a cooked recipe (pie!) or preserved (jam!) or dried (dried mulberries are a personal favorite). But super tart raw fruits, such as cranberries, gooseberries, and currants, are not good to eat raw and better prepared with a little sweetener of your choice.

Preserve any wild fruit by freezing. The frozen product is usually just as good as the fresh fruit for pies, jams, jellies, pancakes, muffins, and smoothies (but with the arguable exception of frozen blueberries, don't add frozen fruit to your fruit salad unless you want a mushy mess). Jams and jellies, of course, are excellent ways to preserve the color and flavor of wild fruit. You can also make syrups to use in cocktails and other beverages, as well as desserts.

Prickly pear (*Opuntia* species) fruit is sweet and juicy, one of the treats of late summer . . . but first you have to get around the glochids.

Most wild fruits dehydrate well. You will preserve more of the color of the fresh fruit if you use a dehydrator (the fruit will darken if oven-dried). Another trick for keeping fruit from browning during dehydration is to first peel and core or pit the fruit, slice it, and then immediately dunk it in a bowl of acidulated water (about a gallon of water with 1 to 2 tablespoons of vinegar or lemon juice added, or ½ teaspoon of citric acid). This step is not necessary for berries, cherries, or plums, but it's great for wild apples, pears, and peaches.

BERRIES

When most people hear the word berry, what comes to mind is a juicy and colorful array of spring and summer fruits that include strawberries, blueberries,

Here I'm wearing a blickey, which leaves both of my hands free for harvesting blueberries.

and blackberries. But actually, only one of the fruits I just named is scientifically considered a berry. A true berry is a simple fruit created in the ovary of a single flower with multiple seeds embedded in the round, juicy pulp. Blueberries, elderberries, gooseberries, juneberries, grapes, cranberries, currants (and—for what it is worth—tomatoes) fit that definition. Strawberries, blackberries, and mulberries do not.

But if I switch to a culinary rather than botanical definition, I find that all of these "berries" have similar preparation and preserving methods, whether you're going for a sweet pie or a savory stew. Since I consider cook just as honorable a title as botanist, I am going with the culinary understanding of berry for this section.

Because they are easily smashed, it's best to use a solid-sided container when you **harvest** berries, rather than a bag. A "blickey" is a useful berry collecting vessel that leaves both of your hands free for picking. To make one, simply punch holes in one side of a plastic container. Alternatively, use a basket. Hook a bungie cord or belt through the holes.

When fully ripe, most berries except cranberry (which is super sour) are delicious straight off the plant. One step from that, add the raw, recently picked berries to fruit salads, pile them on pancakes or whipped cream–based desserts, or add them to smoothies. Besides eating them fresh, all berries are delicious when **prepared** by stewing them with spices into savory-sweet compotes to go with meat or root vegetables, or made into ice cream or sorbet. Beyond that, we're headed into the realm of food preservation, for which all berries are perfectly suited.

The easiest way to **preserve** berries is to freeze them. First spread them out in a single layer on a plate or baking sheet to prevent them from clumping together later. Put the single layer of berries into the freezer for at least 2 hours. Once frozen, transfer them to freezer bags or containers. Small fruits that grow in clusters or umbels, such as elderberries and currants, are best frozen still attached to the cluster. The individual frozen fruits are easier than fresh to roll off their stems without squishing them.

Dehydrate berries in a single layer on dehydrator trays at 135°F until crispy dry. Strawberries larger than ½-inch diameter (rare with wild ones) should be sliced into pieces before dehydrating.

All berries make delicious jam, jelly, and pie. The amount of sweetener, acid, and pectin or starch you need to add to get a thick consistency varies from species to species. Cranberries, for example, are both high pectin and high acidity, so all they need is something to sweeten them. Mulberries, on the other hand, are low pectin and low acidity and need some lemon juice and added pectin to make a good preserve.

BLUEBERRY (*Vaccinium* species)

FIND AND IDENTIFY

Blueberries like acidic soil and often grow near pines and other conifers in mountainous areas. Highbush blueberries (*Vaccinium corymbosum*) can grow as high as 12 feet, although they are usually half that tall. Lowbush blueberries including *V. myrtilloides* and *V. angustifolium* are often no more than 1 foot high.

All blueberry plants have ovate leaves that grow alternately (they join the woody branches singly, not in pairs). When the leaves have petioles (leafstalks) they are very short, or they may not be present at all. Blueberry's small white or pink flowers are easy to identify in spring. Their five petals are fused into a bell or urn-like shape.

Wild blueberries are almost always smaller than cultivated blueberries. But they have the familiar blue to blue-black color, five-pointed crown, and often a whitish bloom on the surface. Blueberries ripen in July and August.

HARVEST

One way to harvest blueberries is to use a special tool called a blueberry rake. A blueberry rake will help you harvest a lot of blueberries faster than picking them by hand. The trouble is that it will harvest some under-ripe fruit and the occasional leaf along with the ripe berries. By the time you sort through and remove those less than desirable bits, you could probably have picked just as many by hand. This is particularly true with highbush blueberries.

Both high- and lowbush varieties of wild blueberries are smaller than cultivated blueberries. But what they lack in size, they make up for in flavor that is much more intense and delightful.

Blueberry rakes are specially made for harvesting blueberries, but it's almost as efficient to do so by hand.

A blickey is very useful when gathering blueberries (see page 128). Blueberries often grow in bear territory, so making a lot of noise to ward them off is a good idea. Singing as loudly as possible while you gather is recommended.

You are not harming the plants by harvesting the berries, but leave some for the wildlife to enjoy, too.

PREPARE

Fresh blueberries are so good on their own that I almost feel I don't need to give you any preparation instructions. But if you've gathered a bumper crop, put them in your pancakes, on yogurt, in muffins, make blueberry pie. Anything you can do with a cultivated blueberry you can do with a wild blueberry, except that the flavor will be vastly better.

PRESERVE

Wild blueberries make fantastic jam. They also dehydrate well. And they are one of the best fruits for freezing (put frozen blueberries straight into your pancake or muffin batter and they will hold their shape in the finished recipe better than if you defrost them first).

It is also possible to can blueberries without any added sugar or liquid. Tie a cup or pint of berries up in cheesecloth and immerse in boiling water for less than a minute, until some purple juice stains start to show on the cheesecloth. Transfer the berries (without the cheesecloth) to a clean half pint or pint canning jar and screw on the lid. Repeat with more blueberries and jars. Process in a boiling water bath (page 262) for 15 minutes.

BRAMBLEBERRIES (*Rubus* species)

HARVEST

Blackberries, raspberries, black raspberries, purple-flowering raspberries, wineberries—all of these scrumptious summer fruits are in the genus *Rubus* and often referred to as "brambleberries." These are plants that form thickets of arching, usually prickly canes. Although they are commercially grown in full sun, when growing wild they usually prefer partial sun edge habitats. Look for them at the edges of meadows and along roadsides.

Purple flowering raspberry (*Rubus odoratus*) is not as well-known as red and black raspberries, but it has good flavor and deserves to be used more.

Most brambleberries have compound, toothed leaves (purple-flowering raspberry, with its maple-shaped leaves is an exception). The pink or white flowers have the multiple pollen-tipped stamens typical of this plant family (Rosaceae). Brambleberries drop their leaves and die back for the winter, regrowing from the perennial roots the following spring.

Although a bit of sourness is an attractive part of the flavor profile of these berries, they should be ripe enough to practically drop into your hand. Any that require even a light tug are going to be too sour or even astringent.

I'm supposed to tell you to wear long pants and long sleeves so that the prickles (often incorrectly dubbed "thorns") don't get you. But let's face it, these fruits ripen during the warmest months of the year and I, at least, am more comfortable in shorts and a tank top at that time of year. If I know I've got bramble berries on my agenda and am headed to a particular patch, I may follow that advice and cover up. But regardless, during the brambleberry months, I have a thick garden or work glove in my knapsack. Yes, you read that correctly: glove, singular. You'll be using that gloved hand to pull the prickly canes toward you while the other, bare and therefore more sensitive, hand picks the berries. If possible, wear a blickey to drop the fruit into so that both your gloved and ungloved hands are free to pick berries.

Some foragers swear by PVC berry pickers, but I am not a fan. A PVC berry picker is a length of plastic tube that has been shaped (with the help of a saw and a blow torch) into tines or "claws" on one end. This is used to rake the berries into the tube and then collect them in a bag that is attached to the other end of the tube. The trouble is that while they extend your reach and protect your hands and arms, they are not as sensitive as your bare fingers when it comes to gathering only fully ripe fruit.

Brambleberry leaves are a decent tea ingredient. While not aromatic, their tannins give infusions some of the mouthfeel of "true" tea (*Camellia sinensis*). I dry some to mix with mint, spicebush, or other aromatics for comforting winter brews that are also good for sore throats and digestive troubles.

PREPARE
All ripe brambleberries are delicious raw, and make excellent jam, wine, and pie. They are also great in sauces and conserves to go with meat and poultry (think cranberry sauce for the turkey, only better).

PRESERVE
Brambleberries freeze well. Freeze them in a single layer on a baking sheet or plates first, then transfer to freezer bags or containers. Frozen bramble berries can be added directly to smoothies, pancakes, muffins, and jam recipes without thawing.

The aforementioned wine and jam are also classic ways to preserve these fruits.

BLACKBERRY (*Rubus allegheniensis, R. flagellaris*)

I'd like to think that everyone learned how to identify a wild blackberry as a kid. I'd like to think that you didn't come home with much because you'd eaten most of the berries straight off the plant, still hot from the summer sun. But experience has taught me that sadly many people nowadays are not 100 percent certain what this easy-to-identify berry looks like. Here's what you need to know.

FIND AND IDENTIFY

Like other plants in the *Rubus* genus, blackberry grows on thorny, arching canes. The leaves have three to seven leaflets each and are green on their upper surface and paler green or even silvery white on their undersides. When the wind blows, the leaves will flutter their pale undersides at you, making it easy to spot blackberry plants even from a distance. Blackberries fruit best in full sun, but they frequently grow in partial sun at woodland and rural property edges.

Note that *Rubus flagellaris* is often called blackberry, but it has a low, ground-cover growth habit rather than the several-feet-long canes of *R. allegheniensis*. *R. flagellaris* is also known as dewberry. Both species have five-petaled white flowers with numerous stamens in the center, and grow up to 1 inch in diameter.

Almost everyone is familiar with the cultivated blackberry. Wild blackberries look the same, although sometimes a bit smaller. The berries look like lots of tiny bubbles stuck together (called an aggregate fruit, for my fellow botany enthusiasts). Blackberries come off the plant with the core attached, so they are solid rather than hollow like the closely related raspberry.

Like other brambleberries, blackberries do not ripen all at the same time so you will find white, pink, red, and deep purple fruits all on the same canes.

HARVEST

Because blackberries and other brambleberries do not ripen all at the same time, you'll want to visit productive patches repeatedly over several weeks to maximize your harvest.

If you've already got a blackberry patch scoped out, and you know it's the right time of summer to go picking, then suit up with long pants and a long-sleeved shirt to protect yourself from the thorns. If, as I've mentioned earlier, you find yourself in less protective, more summery clothes, don't worry. Just be sure that in summer your foraging knapsack always includes at least one gardening glove and a container that can be attached around your waist (a blickey). The gloved hand can grab the thorny canes and pull them close while the bare hand plucks the juicy berries and drops them into the container.

Blackberries can be quite invasive, and in any case you are not harming the plants by harvesting the fruits. If you don't have a glove, you can also use a berry hook. Use a hooked walking cane or a long branch with a twig coming off at an angle at one end (forming a hook) to pull a berry-loaded cane toward you.

Often even people who don't think they have ever foraged have at least picked a few black-berries, which are easy to identify and widespread.

Only pick blackberries that are so darkly purple that they are, indeed, almost black. They should come easily off the plant without tugging. Although a bit of acidity is part of the delicious wild blackberry taste, if you need to tug, or the berry is still red, it will be unpleasantly sour.

PREPARE
Like other brambleberries, blackberries make fantastic jam, pie, wine, cordial, and sauces to go with meat or roasted vegetables.

PRESERVE
Blackberries freeze well. Blackberry jam, jelly, wine, and cordial are other great ways to preserve this fruit. They do not dehydrate well in my opinion.

RULE BREAKER

MULBERRY (*Morus* species)

Whenever somebody tells me that they found a "blackberry tree," I know they really found a mulberry tree. The berries do look similar, with their juicy, multiple fruits. Although this plant should technically go in the tree fruits section, the "blackberry tree" mistake is so common that I'm making it a rule breaker to the brambleberries.

FIND AND IDENTIFY

Mulberry trees can grow as tall as 60 feet but are usually quite a bit smaller. They often have three leaf shapes on the same tree: a three-lobed leaf, a two-lobed mitten-shaped leaf, and an almost heart-shaped leaf. (When mulberry trees do not have the variable leaf shapes, the leaves are heart shaped or pointed ovals.) Sassafras also has all three leaf shapes on the same tree, but mulberry leaves are noticeably toothed unlike the smooth edges of sassafras leaves. Mulberry tree leaves grow in an alternate arrangement.

The bark on mulberry trees is a rusty to gray-brown color. On mature trees, it is rough and craggy with vertical ridges. Mulberry tree trunks are short, with the lower branches fairly near the ground. The appearance of the tree when seen from a distance can be somewhat disheveled, with branches sticking out at odd angles. Mulberry fruit ripens from mid-spring through early summer.

The fruit resembles an elongated blackberry (although depending on species and even different cultivars within one species, a ripe mulberry's color may range from deep purple to pale pink-tinged white). Mulberries don't ripen all at once, so it's common to see green, white, pink, and deep purple fruit all on the same branch.

If you've got a mulberry tree on your property, I don't need to tell you when the berries are ready to harvest. They will fall from the tree in large amounts, and if you've got a dark-fruited species, they will stain the ground and pavement they land on. They are too often despised by homeowners who don't realize that they are cursing a delicious fruit that is one of the first to ripen each year.

The most efficient way to gather mulberries is to lay down a drop cloth and shake the branches. The ripe fruit will fall to the ground but not be damaged by the fall. If you don't have a drop cloth with you when you happen upon ripe mulberries, you can pick them straight off the branch. But only collect the

Mulberries, picked or fallen, always come off the tree with a bit of stem attached.

The cloth we used for this mulberry harvest was a bit small for the job, but we made it work by moving it around the tree incrementally as we shook down the different branches.

ones that fall easily into your hand: if you have to tug, the berry is not ripe. Mulberry leaves are edible too; gather when they are in the glossy, translucent, newly unfurled stage.

PREPARE

Mulberries always come off the tree with a little bit of the skinny stem still attached. I usually just ignore these little stems and eat them along with the berry, but if they bother you go ahead and remove them. Mulberries are good raw, made into jam or chutney, pie, pancakes, muffins, homemade wine, vinegar for a fruity salad dressing, and I'm sure many other uses. Let me know what you do with them! Young mulberry leaves can be stuffed like grape leaves, or shredded and added to salads.

PRESERVE

Mulberries are excellent frozen or dehydrated. Note that if you want to remove the little stems for a recipe, the easiest way to do this is to freeze the mulberries first. You will be able to snap off the stems without smashing the berries. Mulberry jam and mulberry chutney are delicious.

TREE FRUITS

From crabapple to hawthorn to persimmon, tree and shrub fruits are among the most abundant wild fruits of summer and autumn.

Stone Fruits

Stone fruits grow on trees or shrubs and each fruit has a single, large seed. These are mid-summer through early autumn crops. Usually we call those large single seeds "pits." Plums, silverberries, cornelian cherries, black cherries, peaches, and apricots are all in this category. Often such fruits are feral, growing on abandoned property or from a pit tossed out after a picnicker's lunch. Other times, as with beach plums (*Prunus maritima*) and black cherry (*Prunus serotina*), they are fully wild.

You are not damaging the tree or shrub by **harvesting** the fruit. Likely other animals besides you are also interested in the fruits, so avoid stripping any single tree or shrub bare. Unlike multi-seeded tree fruits, which are some-times better harvested under-ripe and ripened off the tree (pears are the best example of this), single-seeded tree fruits are at their best when they've fully ripened on the parent plant. An under-ripe peach, for example, will soften and color up if left out at room temperature, but it will never sweeten or become truly juicy once off the tree.

Stone fruits are excellent fresh (if ripe). They are also **prepared** as pies, jams, and wines.

Along with turning stone fruit into jams and wines—both great ways to **preserve** most fruit—they also freeze well (remove the pits before freezing), and some are good dehydrated (especially plums, peaches, and apricots). They make excellent fruit leathers. Dehydrating slightly under-ripe stone fruits concentrates whatever sugar they contain and often improves their flavor (although they will never taste like their fully ripe potential).

These crabapples are not quite fully ripe. At this stage, they were too astringent to be tasty. But a month later they made excellent jelly.

WILD AMERICAN PLUM (*Prunus americana*)

FIND AND IDENTIFY

The wild American plum grows in full sun to partial shade in central and eastern North America. It can grow to be 15 to 25 feet tall, but don't be surprised if you find it smaller. Its form varies from a single-trunked tree to a multi-trunked shrub. When it takes the shrub form, the wild American plum suckers freely and forms colonies. The smaller branches are sometimes thorny.

The eye-catching, five-petaled white flowers appear in clusters in early spring before the 3- to 4-inch leaves emerge (*Prunus americana* is deciduous, meaning it drops its leaves in the fall). The olfactory impact of the flowers is not as pretty as the visual (they smell weird to me). The plums are smaller than most cultivated varieties, usually not more than an inch in diameter. They have reddish skins and bright yellow pulp, with the single "stone" or "pit" typical of this genus. The skin of the fruit frequently has a whitish bloom that can be rubbed off. This bloom is made of wild yeasts, which have many uses.

Note that many feral plums ranging in color from blush to dark purple with varying fruit sizes can be found across North America in gardening zones 3 through 8. They all have edible fruit, although sometimes the fruits are too astringent to be tasty.

HARVEST

It's best to pick wild plums from the branches because they split and bruise easily when they fall to the ground. But you shouldn't have to tug: the fruit will almost fall into your hand when ripe. Wild American plums ripen in early summer. When they start dropping fruit, that is the time to go pick.

With their rosy exteriors and bright yellow, juicy pulp, wild plums are delicious raw but also make great jam and fruit leather.

PREPARE

The quality of wild plums varies from tree to tree. Some have a pleasant mix of sweet and tangy flavors and a deliciously juicy texture when eaten raw. Others may be less juicy and are better once cooked into a jam or made into fruit leather.

PRESERVE

Wild plums make excellent jam, jelly, compote, and fruit leather. You can also take advantage of the wild yeasts present on the surface of most wild plums by using them to jump-start fermentations ranging from soda to pickles to wine.

Multi-Seeded Tree and Shrub Fruits

Multi-seeded tree and shrub fruits include apple, crabapple, pear, hawthorn, pawpaw, and persimmon. Look down, not up, to find out when to **harvest** these fruits. They will start to drop to the ground in mid-summer through early fall depending on location. Don't be concerned if the fruits seem too hard when you first gather them: they will "ripen" (or at least soften) if stored at room temperature.

A drop cloth is a good way to harvest these fruits in quantity. Simply shake the branches over your drop cloth, and then transfer the fruit to containers or bags. A hooked cane, or a branch with a sturdy twig coming off one end at an angle, can be handy for snagging and shaking higher-up branches. If you've come upon a lot of windfall fruit, a dustpan is helpful for scooping it up. Do check your fruit, especially if it has spent some time on the ground, for small holes and signs of worm damage.

The wild versions of apples and pears often leave something to be desired when it comes to texture. And hawthorn fruits are generally mealy. But this doesn't mean their flavor isn't excellent. If the fruit you've found has good flavor but dubious texture, **prepare** it as a purée such as applesauce and pear butter, or make wine or jelly or juice. In addition to the **preservation** methods already mentioned, most wild tree fruits make good fruit leathers. Dehydrated, they are worthy additions to cereal, trail mix, and winter compotes.

WILD APPLE (*Malus* species)

FIND AND IDENTIFY

Growing up to 30 feet tall (but often smaller), apple trees have scaly, rough gray bark. The alternate, oval, pointy-tipped leaves are 2 to 3½ inches long with finely toothed edges. Their undersides are slightly fuzzy. Apple flowers are white or pink, fragrant, and have five petals. They are usually less than 1½ inches in diameter.

Wild apples range from sweet to super tart and have just as many culinary uses as the cultivated fruit.

Wild apple fruits look pretty much like cultivated ones except that they are usually smaller and often slightly misshapen. Cut an apple in half crosswise and you will see that its five seeds are arranged in a pentacle-like pattern. Hawthorn, which has similar-looking fruit, has an inconsistent number of seeds and lacks the pentacle pattern in cross-section.

The flavor of wild apples is so varied because apples do not breed true from seed—if you plant a seed from a Macintosh apple, for example, you have no idea what you will get but it will not be a Macintosh apple. (All cultivated apples are propagated from cuttings, not seeds.)

HARVEST

You can pluck wild apples from the tree, or gather the windfall below the tree. Remember to inspect the fruit for insect damage. Unless the tree is diseased (alas, not uncommon with wild apple trees—you'll be able to tell by the rust-colored spots on the leaves), a good signal that the fruit is ready to pick is when you start seeing windfall apples on the ground below the tree. As with all fruit, you are not harming the parent plant by gathering the fruit.

PREPARE

Sometimes wild apples are as sweet as their cultivated kin, but more often they are extremely tart. Eat the sweet ones straight off the tree, or turn them into pie or anything you would do with a sweet cultivated apple.

Cut away any small bruises and damaged spots. What remains will still be good for chutney and other recipes that use chopped fruit. The tart ones make terrific cider and are high in pectin and great for jam and jelly. You can combine them with low-pectin fruit such as blackberries to get a good gel.

PRESERVE

In addition to cider and jelly, wild apples make good fruit butter, chutney, and fruit leather. For sweeter wild apples, drop slices into acidulated water to minimize discoloration before deyhdrating.

SUMAC (*Rhus typhina*, *R. glabra*, *R. coriaria*, *R. aromatica*)

Here is a delicious fruit that you don't actually eat. Foragers are interested in neither the drupes (fruits) nor their rock-hard seeds but rather the vibrantly sour and brightly colored acid that clings to the fuzz surrounding the drupes.

FIND AND IDENTIFY

Sumac grows on several continents in sunny locations, frequently in rocky soil or dry, disturbed soil habitats such as alongside highways. The shrubs or small trees can get as tall as 25 feet but are usually much shorter.

Sumacs have alternate, pointed, compound leaves with toothed margins. Those leaves turn a fiery scarlet in the fall. The small, yellow-green flowers grow in Christmas tree–shaped clusters. Sumac's rusty red, conical, fuzzy fruit clusters made up of multiple small, round, hard-seeded nodules are conspicuous and easy to spot from mid- to late summer, the ideal harvest time. They hang on through winter, turning almost black as the weather chills and the leaves drop from the branches.

Sumac's fuzzy clusters make both a liquid extract and a dry spice. Both are colorful and fabulously tangy.

HARVEST

The vivid color and mouthwatering sourness of sumac is at its peak in mid- to late summer when the fuzzy fruit clusters turn a deep, rusty red color—and when it hasn't rained recently. In regions where summer thundershowers are common, it can be tricky to catch the sumac harvest at just the right time. Rain washes away the acid on the surface of the fruit clusters that gives sumac its wonderfully tart flavor.

I could tell you to wait three days after a rain, or four days, or a week (common foraging advice), but no matter what you'll need to taste test in the field to be certain your sumac is worth harvesting. This is true even in arid regions where degree of ripeness is the issue instead of rain. I used to simply lick one of the clusters to determine if it was worth harvesting from that sumac shrub on that particular day. But then it occurred to me that if I did not harvest, subsequent foragers might not appreciate that I'd already partaken (not that they would know, but . . .). Now I pull off a few fruits from the cluster, or one whole cluster, and give it a lick. If it is good and sour, start harvesting.

I like to use pruners to cleanly and easily cut off the whole drupes, but it is possible to snap or twist them off. Harvest the edible shoots anytime that the stems are a solid green with no whitish pith. Sumac can be invasive, and harvesting the fruit clusters or a few shoots in no way endangers the plant.

PREPARE

Sumac gives foragers two pleasantly sour and colorful ingredients: a liquid extract and a dry, powdered spice. For either of those preparations, first remove any leaves and give the clusters a good shake to dislodge other debris and insects.

For the liquid extract, fill a bowl with room-temperature water, rub apart several of the sumac clusters by hand (in the water), and let them soak for at least 30 minutes before straining and adding a new batch of sumac clusters to the already infused

The bright red color of this sumac-ade, as well as its tangy taste, comes naturally from the fuzzy drupes.

POISON SUMAC

When I point out edible sumacs on my foraging tours, someone always asks, "But isn't there a poison sumac?" Yes, there is: *Toxicodendron vernix*. It is not in the same genus as the edible sumacs, and has white, drooping fruit clusters rather than the more or less upright, rusty red clusters of *Rhus* fruit.

liquid and repeating the procedure. Yes, your fingers will get sticky. Other forager friends use different methods to make their "sumac-ade," but this is what works best for me.

For the dried spice, dry whole sumac fruit clusters in paper or cloth bags. Rub the fruits off the central stems. Pulse them in a food processor (don't worry: the seeds are too tough to succumb to the processor). Rub the result through a fine-mesh sieve. The deep red, delightfully sour powder will come through leaving the flavorless seeds behind.

PRESERVE

Preserve liquid sumac extract by freezing it in ice cube trays, then transferring the sumac cubes to a freezer bag or container. Thaw the cubes and use them instead of lemon juice in salad dressings and marinades, or as a fascinating cocktail addition.

Sprinkle dried sumac spice over any dish that could use a hit of tangy flavor and red color. It is part of the za'atar blend that is ubiquitous in the Middle East, and commonly used as a flavoring and garnish in North Africa.

If you've harvested a lot of sumac clusters and don't have time to process them right away, you can either freeze or dry them.

ROSE HIPS (*Rosa* species)

Yeah, I know, this is two rule breakers in a row. But rose hips are just as much in their own category as sumac. The fruit of the rose—called a "hip" rather than a berry or other kind of fruit—would not be tasty if you just popped it into your mouth for a snack. It has a hairy center that you have to scrape out. But it is so worth it.

FIND AND IDENTIFY

Rose plants have compound leaves with an odd number of leaflets per leaf and toothed leaflet margins. They grow alternately on prickly shrubs or canes. Scientifically speaking, roses don't have thorns: they have prickles. The difference is that true thorns come out of the wood of the plant (for example, hawthorn) and do not break off easily, whereas prickles come from the outer layers and snap off easily.

Unlike florist shop roses, wild roses rarely have the dense cluster of multiple petals we've come to think of as "a rose." Instead, they are often a single circle of petals with multiple pollen-tipped stamens at the center (the multiple stamens are a key identifier of the plant family Rosaceae). Pink and white are the most common colors for wild rose flowers. Each flower has a pointy, green calyx at its base that remains once the flower turns into the fruit.

Once the rose petals drop from the flower, the base of the flower starts to swell. By late summer or early autumn, the orb the flower base has become will turn bright orange or red. They can range in diameter from ¼ inch to as large as 1 inch. They almost always have a five-pointed crown at one end.

Roses like full sun but will tolerate partial sunlight. Feral roses often appear near abandoned farms and gardens. Salt-tolerant roses such as *Rosa rugosa* are commonly planted by landscapers at beachside properties and roadways.

HARVEST

Before harvesting the flowers, smell them. No smell? No taste. The same essential oils that give the petals their pollinator-attracting fragrance give them the flavor that is famously used in North African cuisines. If they are richly perfumed they are worth gathering: simply pinch off the flowers into a cloth or

Rose hips—the fruit of the rose plant—can be harvested well into winter. In fact, they are tastier after a few freezes.

paper bag. Harvest the leaves anytime they are green and healthy looking (i.e., not afflicted by black spot or other fungal diseases). The hips, or fruit of the rose, are ready when they are bright red or orange. Simply snap or snip them off.

PREPARE

For tea, wine, or jelly—any preparation where the solids will be strained out— you can simply lightly smash whole rose hips and use them fresh or dried. But if the pulp is going to be part of the final recipe, you'll need to remove the hairy, seedy center that is present in any rose hips that are large enough to bother harvesting (½ inch or more in diameter). To do this, cut them in half and then use a serrated grapefruit spoon or other small spoon to scrape out the center part.

If you are planning to eat the fragrant rose flowers as part of a salad or other dish where you will directly chew the flower, remove the petals from the flower centers. If the flowers will be infused and then strained out of a base (water, alcohol, honey, syrup), just leave them whole.

Rose leaves can be used for tea fresh or dried so long as they don't show signs of fungal disease such as black spot (very common on rose plants).

PRESERVE

Preserve rose hips by dehydrating or freezing them. Either way, scoop out the fuzzy core first (it will be nearly impossible to do so once they are frozen or dried). You can also make wine or jam using fresh, dried, or frozen rose hips.

10

SEEDS, NUTS, AND PODS

I KNOW, I KNOW: nuts, and the beans within pods, *are* technically seeds, so why not just call this chapter "Seeds"? The reason is that the gathering and processing methods for small seeds, nuts, and pods are very different. Whatever you call them, these foods are loaded with nutrition and flavor. Designed to create the next generation of plants, they house a store of protein, carbohydrates, and other nutrients that have made them prized ingredients for thousands of years.

SEEDS

The type of wild seeds I'm talking about here—such as garlic mustard, evening primrose, plantain, lamb's quarters, and dock—are so small that you can fit hundreds in the palm of your hand. They are packed with nutrients and have flavors that range from spicy enough to use as a seasoning (mustard seeds, for example) to mild enough to use as a flour or cooked into porridge (amaranth).

Don't be intimidated by their small size. Gathering these kinds of wild seeds isn't difficult, and the yield can be abundant enough to warrant your effort. Once you've gathered and processed them, you can turn them into flour, crunchy casserole toppings and cereal ingredients, salad sprouts, and even porridge for an oatmeal-like breakfast or a polenta-style dinner.

Notice that I didn't mention grains. Usually the word "grains" refers to the seeds of plants in the Poaceae, or grass, family. Our cultivated grains (wheat, corn, barley, etc.) are in that family. Most wild grass seeds are a pain to harvest in any quantity, although foxtail grass (*Alopecurus*) is an exception and worth the time.

Small Seeds Easily Separated from Chaff

Most small wild seeds including amaranth, mallow, mustard, lamb's quarters, dock, evening primrose, and garlic mustard are easily separated from the chaff. *Chaff* is a catchall term that describes papery husks, stem fragments, and any plant part surrounding or connected to the seed (in other words, all of the parts that you usually need to remove from the edible seed). All the plants I just mentioned are considered invasive, so it is a bonus that this method minimizes the inadvertent spread of seeds while you are collecting.

To **harvest** these small seeds, place a cloth or paper bag upside down over the upper stalks of the plant where the seed heads are. Close the bag below the seed heads that are now inside the bag. Grasp the bag with one hand so that the open end is tightly wrapped around the seed head stalks. With your other hand, use scissors or pruners to cut off the stalks. You are now holding something like a bouquet of seeds, except that they are hidden inside of the bag. Secure the bottom of your "bouquet" with string or a rubber band.

Preparing small seeds that are easily separated from their chaff involves a couple of steps:

Mallow (*Malva*) is better known for its edible leaves and immature seed heads, but the ripe seeds can thicken sauces and desserts.

Dry

Leave the seed heads to dry in the bags for at least a week in a place with good air circulation and, if possible, low humidity. Be sure the bags are not plastic, or the seed heads could mold instead of drying. Before opening the bag, crush it gently with your hands or a rolling pin. (Note: for evening primrose [*Oenothera biennis*] seeds, don't be so gentle—the pods need a little more pressure to crack open.)

Winnow

Open the bag and dump its contents into a large bowl. If it is a breezy day, take the bowl outside for the next step. If there is no breeze, you can use a fan. But remember that the chaff is going to blow everywhere, so you may want to set up an extension cord and take the fan outside. Rub the seed heads with your hands, crushing them one more time to release any seeds that didn't come

Wild mustard seeds and what is left of the narrow pods called siliques that enclosed them.

loose in the bag. Remove any stalks, leaves, or other large debris from the bowl. (Be careful how you dispose of these: the seed heads of invasive plants such as garlic mustard should not be composted or next year you'll just be spreading that plant.) Now you've got a mix of seeds and chaff in the bottom of your bowl.

Lift a handful of the chaff and seeds about a foot high over the bowl. Slowly let the seeds fall back into the bowl. The wind (or fan) will blow the chaff away, while the seeds, which are heavier, fall back into the bowl. Repeat until the seeds are chaff-free. With very small seeds, it may be also possible to dump them into a fine-mesh sieve. Shake the sieve over a bowl. If the seeds are small enough and the sieve's holes are not too large, the seeds should fall through into the bowl, leaving the chaff behind.

To **prepare** small, mildly flavored wild seeds such as amaranth and lamb's quarters, you can boil them into porridge; grind them into flour; or lightly toast them in a dry pan and then add to baked goods, sprout them, or even pop them.

You can use sprouted wild seeds as salad and sandwich ingredients. This is an excellent way to turn a few spoonfuls of wild seeds into enough food to make a significant contribution to a healthy meal. Wild sprouts will add a light crunch to your food, with flavors that range from lettuce-like (lamb's quarters) to a radish-like pungency (evening primrose).

Popping wild seeds is a bit different from making popcorn. For starters, don't use any oil. Place no more than two tablespoons of wild seeds into a pot over medium-high heat. Put on the lid and shake the pot constantly to prevent the seeds from burning. You'll hear them start to pop. When that merry sound slows down, remove the pot from the heat and transfer the popped seeds to a bowl or container. Proceed with as many batches as you like. If your seeds burn rather than pop, either the heat was too high or too many were seeds crowded in the pot.

Dry wild seeds are already naturally **preserved**, and will keep in closed jars for several months and up to a year. If you plan to use your seeds as flour, it is best to store them whole and grind them when you are ready to use them. Already ground, wild seed flour can turn rancid quickly unless stored at cold temperatures.

AMARANTH (*Amaranthus* species)

FIND AND IDENTIFY
Amaranth plants love full sun and are a common weed in urban areas as well as on farms and in gardens. The plants are annuals that pop up once temperatures are reliably above freezing (mid-spring in most places). All plants in the *Amaranthus* genus have edible seeds and leaves.

Size won't help you identify these excellent wild edibles: species can vary from ground-hugging, sprawling mats to plants as tall as 7 feet. Amaranth's oval leaves have untoothed margins, but some species have a single notch at the tip of the leaf. The leaves grow in an alternate arrangement on the stalks, and have prominent veins. Some amaranth species have a reddish color at the tops of their roots (one of the most common amaranths, *Amaranthus retroflexus*, is called redroot because of this trait). A reddish coloration may be present on the stems and undersides of the leaves, too.

Amaranth seeds were once a staple food of Central and South America.

Amaranth's flowers grow in fuzzy clusters at the tops and/or leaf axils of the plants. Eventually, these clusters turn into tan or brown seed heads. The seeds are miniscule, and usually brown or black (unlike the cream-colored seeds of most cultivated amaranth).

HARVEST

Collect the leaves anytime from when the plants appear in late spring until they start to flower. If the stems are still tender enough to snap easily, go ahead and harvest them with the leaves still attached (they will be good to eat at this stage). I prefer to eat amaranth greens cooked because when raw their texture can be coarse. The flavor is mild. Collect amaranth seeds once the seed heads have changed color from green to tan, and the seeds shake out easily.

PREPARE

You can cook the seeds into porridge, but because of their small size, the result can be somewhat gluey. I prefer to combine amaranth seeds with other seeds or grains. Amaranth seeds are among the best wild seeds for popping, and the popped seeds can be used to give a nutty flavor and light crunch to crackers, salads, granola, and trail mix. They can also be ground into flour.

PRESERVE

Amaranth seeds can be stored in airtight containers for up to 3 months. If you wish to store them for longer than that without fear of them turning rancid, keep them in the refrigerator or freezer. The leaves can be blanched and frozen, or they may be dehydrated.

Small Seeds Not Easily Separated from Chaff

Some plants, including plantain (*Plantago*), peppergrass (*Lepidium*), and dock (*Rumex crispus*, *R. obtusifolius*, and others), have tiny seeds encased in chaff that is hard to remove. With these types of seeds, I don't bother trying to winnow. I just use the flavorless chaff together with the tasty seeds and call it extra fiber.

Peppergrass is a mildly invasive native North American plant in the mustard family. Its immature, still-green seed pods make a horseradish-flavored seasoning.

To **harvest** this type of seed, snip off the seed stalks and place them in a cloth or paper bag. Leave in a dry place with good air circulation for at least a week. With these kinds of seeds, it's up to you whether you prefer to store them still attached to their stalks, or already stripped off and in containers. Since the seeds don't easily fall from the plants, I often store plantain seed stalks or dock or peppergrass seed heads whole in cloth or paper bags. Then I get around to preparing the seeds weeks or even months later.

To **prepare**, strip the seeds (with their chaff) off the stalks. You can hold the tip of a stalk with one hand and gently strip the seeds away with the other hand by moving from the growth tip toward the base of the stalk. Or you can vigorously rub the stalks in a back-and-forth motion to release the seeds and chaff from the stalk. Remove any twigs or dried stalks. You can use the seeds together with their chaff in baked goods and cooked cereal blends, or you can grind them into a flour or spice.

The seeds are better **preserved** if you wait to grind them (and tenacious chaff) until you are ready to use them. Once ground, they can turn rancid rapidly (and peppergrass tends to lose its flavor). If you do want to store already ground seed flour, put it in airtight containers in the refrigerator, freezer, or other cold storage place.

BROAD-LEAVED DOCK (*Rumex obtusifolius*)

Also known as bitter dock, this common weed is often downplayed in the foraging community in favor of its better-known cousin curly dock (*Rumex crispus*). But not only is broad-leaved dock tasty, it is the most common species of "dock" in many regions. Let's put this abundant-to-the-point-of-being-invasive wild vegetable on the table, shall we?

FIND AND IDENTIFY
Broad-leaved dock is an invasive plant that likes disturbed soils such as those we humans create in our parks, gardens, roadsides, and farms. It will grow in both full and partial sunlight. It dies back to the ground each winter and regrows from its perennial roots. The large leaves (4 to 16 inches long) emerge first in a low spiral that resembles a rosette growth habit. The leaves are at least

Broad-leaved dock is a common weed in parks, gardens, and farm fields that provides edible leaves, stalks, and seeds.

twice as long as they are wide but are not as wavily ruffled as the edges of curly dock's usually narrower leaves. The leafstalks and the mid-veins of the leaves are often tinged with red.

The green flowers emerge in clusters at the top of stalks that can be as tall as 3 feet. The leaves on the flower stalks are alternate (attaching to the stalks singly rather than in aligned pairs), and much smaller than the base leaves. As the seeds develop and ripen within rounded, papery sheaths, the clusters turn a deep rusty brown and can be spotted from some distance.

HARVEST

Gather the young leaves during cold weather in early spring or late fall, as the leaves tend to be too bitter for most tastes in warm weather. Look for leaves that still have faint creases running lengthwise. These creases remind me of the temporary wrinkles that show up on my cheek when I've slept on a bunched-up pillowcase. They are signs that the leaf just recently unfurled and will be super tender.

Collect the flower stalks anytime before the flower heads develop. They are mucilaginous and it is helpful to use a small sharp knife to cut them off at the base: trying to snap them off bare-handed can be a slimy process.

Harvest the seeds once the seed heads have turned rusty brown by snipping off entire seed heads as in the general harvesting method described on page 151.

PREPARE

If they are not in their hot weather/bitter stage, the leaves are enjoyable both raw and cooked. They are slightly acidic and pair well with beans and lentils.

Some people enjoy the peeled flower stalks raw, but they are a bit too mucilaginous for my tastes. I prefer to chop and add them to gumbo and other dishes where okra is the more familiar ingredient.

The seeds (by which I mean both the tiny seeds and their surrounding rust-colored chaff) are good ground into flour and made into crackers. I have also successfully added dock flour to bread, although I'm not sure they contributed much flavor.

PRESERVE

Store broad-leaved dock seed heads intact, or strip the seeds from their stalks when fully dry and keep in tightly covered jars. As with other wild seeds, it is better not to grind these into flour until you are ready to use them.

SIBERIAN ELM (*Ulmus pumila*)

Siberian elm is a rule breaker in the seed category because not only do you eat the seed, but you eat the sheath surrounding the seed. And you do so primarily when the seed is still green and far from ripe.

FIND AND IDENTIFY

Because Siberian elm trees are both drought and pollution tolerant, landscapers have planted them widely in urban areas. And then, because these trees drop copious amounts of seeds that have a high germination rate, "volunteer" Siberian elm saplings can usually be found near the intentionally planted parent tree. Look for this tree primarily in sunny urban locations but also at the edges of rural property lines.

All elm trees have alternate, ovate leaves with serrated margins. But Siberian elm's leaves are much smaller than other elm species, usually no more than 1½ to 2½ inches. The trees are smaller than native North American elm species as well, usually not taller than 60 feet but with a wider spread. And Siberian elm's bark is full of craggy chunks, unlike the curved ridges of other elms. It's important to make sure that the tree you want to eat from is indeed Siberian elm, which is delicious, rather than one of the other elm species that are not as tasty and have reportedly caused allergies in some people.

The parts of the Siberian elm tree that you are going to eat are the samaras. A samara is a winged seed (maple "keys," for example, are samaras). Elm samaras are flat discs about ½-inch wide containing a single seed. They appear in light green, ruffled-looking clusters before the leaves emerge in spring. And the samaras offer foragers one last ID clincher: Siberian elm samaras are hairless and have a notch at one end. The samaras of other elms have eyelash-like hairs on their margins and may or may not be notched.

HARVEST

It's easy to gather the immature samaras in quantity by simply stripping them off the branches. They are worth gathering from when they first appear and are completely green through when the papery sheath is still green but the seed at the center is showing some red. The mature samaras will fall to the earth and get blown into noticeable drifts below the tree. The easiest way to collect them is to scoop them up with a dustpan or similarly shaped tool.

Elm samaras appear on the branches before the tree's leaves unfurl in spring.

Siberian elm is considered an invasive "weed tree" in areas where it has been introduced. You are not harming the tree by harvesting the samaras, and you are probably not having much of an impact on the vigorous spread of this species.

PREPARE

Green, immature Siberian elm samaras are delicious raw, straight off the tree. They are also good steamed very briefly (no more than a minute) and served with a little salt. Once they've lost their green color and become dry, the papery seed covering is no longer good to eat. At this stage, rub the samaras vigorously to release the seeds within. You can use the seeds in hot or cold cereals, as a salad topping, or combined with whole grains.

PRESERVE

Mature Siberian elm seeds, with their papery wings removed, can be frozen for future use. Unfortunately, the immature, still-green, whole samaras do not preserve well.

NUTS

Nuts are loaded with protein and healthy fats, and taste so good that "a nutty flavor" is its own category of taste description. These tree products are easy to gather in quantity, and they store well. Nuts have been an important food for humans for tens of thousands of years. And harvesting the nuts that have freely fallen to the ground in no way harms the tree or surrounding environment.

Some of the foods I've included in this section are not really nuts, if you go by the strict scientific definition. Just in case the botany police are on your case, here's that definition: True nuts are pods with firm shells that contain both the seed and the fruit of the tree, and that do not split open to disperse the seed. Examples are acorns, hazelnuts, and chestnuts.

Other foods we call nuts are actually drupes, which have a fleshy outer layer, or husk, surrounding the shell-encased seed. These include walnuts, almonds, butternuts, and hickory nuts. From an eater's point of view, they're all nuts, so that's what I'm calling them here.

Wild nuts, including these acorns, are one of our best and most under-utilized, environmentally friendly protein sources. Harvesting them does not harm the tree, and there are inevitably more than enough left for other nut-eating animals.

Different types of nuts require different techniques to get from the harvest to your meal. In this section, I've outlined how to deal with hard-shelled nuts, soft-shelled nuts, and acorns.

Hard-Shelled Nuts

When I say "hard-shelled," I mean *really* hard. People have been known to deliberately run their cars over these delectable wild foods to crack their tough shells. Hard-shelled nuts include black walnut (*Juglans nigra*), butternut (*J. cinerea*), and hickory nuts (*Carya*). Hard-shelled nuts typically fall from the tree in very late summer and early autumn just as the leaves begin to yellow. They have a fleshy hull that is generally green, and the overall shape may resemble a globe or a football, depending on the species. You can **harvest** by hand or use a Nut Wizard to scoop up the harvest (refer to chapter 3 on page 21 for more about using this tool).

The first step in **preparing** hard-shelled tree nuts is to remove the hulls. You can store hard-shelled nuts in their shells for many months once the hulls are removed. But if you leave the hulls on, they will blacken and release heat as they decompose, changing the color and taste of the nutmeats in unsavory ways. To remove, simply tap each nut with a hammer or rock to crack the green hull, and then pry it off (the hulls are not as tough to crack as the shells they enclose). Stomping on them with the heel of your shoe also works. Be sure to wear gloves when you pry off the cracked hulls since they will stain your hands dark brown ("walnut" furniture stain was originally made from real walnut hulls).

Once the hulls are removed, spread the nuts in a single layer to dry for a couple of weeks before piling them in a basket, bin, or any large container. This step **preserves** the nuts by preventing them from molding while they are in storage. They will store for 1 year at room temperature before they start to turn rancid.

The next step is to remove the shells. It is impossible to do this with a lightweight handheld nutcracker. If you know you will be processing a lot of nuts each year, it is worth investing in a hard-shell nutcracker made specifically for dealing with black walnuts, butternuts, and other hard-shelled nuts. It is also possible to use a hammer or simply smash them with a rock.

When cracking hard-shelled nuts, shell shards can fly everywhere and you end up with quite a mess to clean up. One solution is to lay down a tarp before you get cracking. If you are using a hard-shell nutcracker (or a hammer or

rock), placing a cloth around the nut before cracking prevents shell shrapnel from flying. Another solution is to place the nut in a hollowed-out piece of wood or a basket and crack it there.

Once you've cracked your hard-shelled nuts, you'll need to get the nutmeats out. This is not nearly as easy as it is with cultivated nuts, but a nut-picker, metal skewer, or even the tine of a fork does the job well. You can store the shelled nutmeat in the freezer indefinitely, providing a ready-to-use delicious and nutrient-packed ingredient. But if you are short on freezer space, as I often am, it is better to store them still in their shells because the shelled nuts turn rancid rapidly when stored at room temperature.

Black walnut is a classic example of a hard-shelled nut that requires some work but is well worth it for the excellent food contained within its stubborn shell.

BLACK WALNUT (*Juglans nigra*)

Black walnuts have such a unique, almost minty flavor that they are as much a seasoning as a staple food. With a much stronger taste than cultivated walnuts, they become the dominant (and exquisite) flavor of any recipe they are used in. Black walnut ice cream is a classic example in which the nuts not only add crunch but also infuse their flavor into the entire dessert.

FIND AND IDENTIFY

Black walnut trees grow as tall as 100 feet. They have three-lobed leaf scars on the twigs that leave a mark some have described as a monkey face. The compound leaves are 1 to 2 feet long, alternate, and have 10 to 24 lance-shaped or ovate leaflets. The terminal leaflet is stunted or absent. Each leaflet is around

Black Walnuts start dropping to the ground in late summer and early autumn.

A tool such as the Nut Wizard is by far the easiest way to collect recently fallen nuts (as well as windfall apples).

3 inches long and has serrated margins. The bark is rough with vertical strips that look as if they are trying to form plaits.

Black walnuts fall to the ground with their green hulls still attached, with a size somewhere between a tennis ball and golf ball. Inside the outer green hull is the shell-encased walnut.

Black walnut trees are allelopathic, which means that their roots exude a chemical that discourages other plants from growing nearby. It is common to find few, if any, other plants growing under a black walnut tree.

HARVEST

Gather black walnuts soon after they have fallen to the ground. Wear gloves to avoid staining your fingers brown, or simply pick them up lightly with thumb and forefinger and drop them into your collection vessel. Or avoid the staining issue entirely and use a Nut Wizard.

Black walnuts can be tapped for their sap in late winter and very early spring (see chapter 12 for instructions).

PREPARE

Black walnuts have a texture similar to commercially sold walnuts but a strong, unique flavor that acts as a robust seasoning. In addition to the classic black walnut ice cream, try them in other desserts such as cookies, cakes, and crumbles. They are also excellent in savory stuffing and with cooked grains. Just keep in mind that their flavor will dominate the recipe.

PRESERVE

As with other hard-shelled nuts, black walnuts should be dried for a couple of weeks (still in their shells) after the hulls are removed. Once shelled, it is best to freeze the nutmeats.

Thin-Shelled Nuts

Thin-shelled nuts, such as hazelnuts, chestnuts, and beechnuts, can be easily cracked open with a handheld nutcracker or a pocket knife. Acorns also fit this category, but they have such a high tannin content that they need a radically different preparation method. Because of this, I handle acorns in a separate section.

As soon as you see that some nuts have dropped, **harvest** by laying out a tarp and shaking the branches. More ripe nuts will fall off the tree or shrub (hazelnuts tend to be more firmly attached and can be picked off the shrubs by hand). Remove any outer layers (the papery involucres of hazelnuts, for example, or the prickly hulls of chestnuts and beechnuts) and then crack open your thin-shelled nuts.

You can eat these nuts raw, or **prepare** them by toasting in a dry skillet or briefly baking, then chopping and adding them to desserts, cereal, homemade energy bars, salads, pasta, and pretty much anything else. You can also grind them to make nut butters, or make your own nut milks (see page 170).

All thin-shelled nuts will keep for several months stored in their shells, longer if frozen. Remove any outer coverings, including involucres (the papery sheath around hazelnuts) and cups (on acorns), and rinse the nuts well with water before storing. The rinsing will help remove mold spores, which will help to **preserve** your nuts in good eating condition.

After rinsing, the nuts should be dried to reduce the chance of mold developing while they are in storage. You are just trying to dry off the surfaces of the nuts, not actually drying the nutmeats themselves, so there is no need to pull out the dehydrator or stick them into the oven. Simply spread them in a single layer on any flat surface that will be easy to transport if you need to move the nuts from outdoors to indoors. This could be rimmed cookie sheets, the lids of plastic bins—whatever works. It is important that the nuts remain dry during this step. That means that if you are drying them outdoors, you will need to bring them in at night so that they don't get coated with dew. You can also set the trays of nuts next to a woodstove or fire, or even just in a dry, warm room with good air circulation.

After 2 weeks, you can pile the nuts into any container and store them in a dry, cool place such as your refrigerator or freezer (or an unheated garage if you live in a cold winter climate).

AMERICAN HAZELNUT (*Corylus americana*)

FIND AND IDENTIFY

American hazelnuts ripen in late summer and early autumn. Look for them in full sun to partial shade, often at the edges of clearings. In the wild, hazelnut shrubs frequently form colonies (cultivated hazelnuts are pruned to prevent this). Although they can grow as tall as 16 feet and as wide as 13 feet, they are usually smaller.

Hazelnut's ovate leaves are between 3 and 6 inches long and half as wide. They grow alternately (joining the branches singly rather than in aligned pairs). The edges are serrated, and the bases somewhat heart shaped. In autumn, hazelnut leaves turn a dull yellow or a more eye-catching copper-red. Both male and female flowers appear on the shrubs in spring. Male hazelnut flowers are showy, yellow-brown cattails that grow up to 3 inches long. Female hazelnut flowers are smaller and reddish.

It is the female flowers that turn into the prized nuts. Wild hazelnuts are smaller than some cultivated ones. They are usually about ½ inch in diameter.

The frilly, paper sheathes (called involucres) that surround American hazelnuts make this wonderful wild edible easy to identify.

What makes them especially easy to identify, assuming the other ID characteristics line up, is the light green to tan papery sheath that encloses each nut as if it was gift wrapped. These sheaths, called involucres, are frilly and flared at one end.

HARVEST

Before you start gathering hazelnuts, peel back the involucres from a couple of them. When ripe, the nuts will be either fully brown or at least showing some brown coloration. If they're still green, they are not ready (but note that sometimes the involucres are still greenish even when the nuts are ripe).

Pick them by hand off the shrubs. Spread them out in a single layer in a dry place with their involucres still attached and let them dry out for a day or two. This brief drying period makes it easier to remove the ruffled wrappings afterward.

MAKING NUT MILK FROM UNSHELLED NUTS

Here is one more way of turning wild nuts into a terrific ingredient that does not require shelling the nuts.

1 part nuts

3 to 4 parts water

To make creamy, naturally rich vegan nut milk, all you need to do is pound the hulled and washed nuts, then simmer them in water for about 20 minutes. Use the smaller amount of water for a creamier result, and more for a lighter nut milk. Remove from the heat and let the nutmeats and shells settle to the bottom. Ladle off the nut milk above the solids.

Note: This method only works with nuts that do not have a high tannin content or dye-rich hulls. So far, I have only tried it with hickory nuts and hazelnuts.

Freshly made hazelnut milk is strained through cloth to remove solids including shell bits.

PREPARE

Strip the involucres off the hazelnuts. Drop the nuts into a bucket or pot of water. Discard any "floaters" (hazelnuts that float to the top have been bored into by insects and are worthless to you). The nuts that sank to the bottom of your water-filled vessel are your keepers. Drain the nuts, spread them out in a single layer, and leave in a dry place for 2 to 7 days (this will prevent mold). Transfer to storage containers.

Hazelnuts are easy to crack with an ordinary handheld nutcracker from the supermarket or with a firm tap of a rock or hammer. The nuts are delicious freshly shelled, or in any recipe that uses cultivated hazelnuts. They are heavenly in pie crusts or sprinkled on top of baked fruit crumbles. Try them in savory recipes such as stuffing as well. Hazelnuts also make one of my favorite wild nut milks (see Making Nut Milk box).

PRESERVE

After drying them in a single layer for a few days to a week, store still-in-their-shell American hazelnuts in containers that allow good air circulation (baskets, or cloth or paper bags). They will last for several months this way. Eat shelled hazelnuts within a few days or freeze for future use.

Acorns

Although acorns are indeed thin-shelled (and soft-shelled) nuts, they are rule breakers because unlike other soft-shelled nuts, they have to go through a leaching process to remove their tannins before they are edible.

RULE BREAKER

ACORNS (*Quercus* species)

Acorns are such a versatile and nutritious ingredient that they have been a staple food on four continents despite being labor-intensive to prepare. Oak trees, and the acorns from those trees, have been used as food in all the places where they grow: North America, Europe, Asia, and northern Africa. In fact, in parts of Asia, acorn flour and starch are sold as a commercial product (the

Korean acorn jelly *dotorimuk* is delicious, and worth learning to make from your own wild acorn starch).

FIND AND IDENTIFY

Acorns are the fruits of oak trees (botanically speaking a fruit is simply the seed-bearing part of a plant, so nuts count as fruits). Large oak species usually grow as one of the predominant species in deciduous forests. Small oaks with a more shrub-like growth habit can be found on sunny hills and often in rocky soils. And landscapers frequently plant oaks in parks, backyards, and as street trees.

Whether tall and stately or small and scrubby, all members of the *Quercus* genus have alternate, leathery leaves that are usually lobed. Those species called white oaks have rounded lobes, whereas the lobes of red and black oaks are sharply pointed. There are also oaks that have toothed but unlobed, holly-shaped leaves. Oaks have male and female dangling flowers that are yellow-green and often described as "inconspicuous." You'll notice them most when they pile on the ground under the oak tree in the spring.

The acorns—the edible nuts people have eaten for millennia—are sometimes shaped like 2-inch-long and ½-inch-wide bullets, sometimes round and more than 1 inch in diameter, sometimes small and squat. Whichever shape they take, all acorns have thin, brown shells nested in a detachable "cup" or cap.

Oak trees don't produce acorns consistently every year. They have "mast years," in which they produce copious amounts of nuts, but the next year they may produce far less.

HARVEST

Collect acorns soon after they fall from the tree in late summer and early fall. The longer they stay on the ground, the more likely that squirrels and grubs are going to get to them. Inspect each acorn before you drop it into your collection vessel to make sure that it does not have any small holes, which are a sign that insects already got to that nut. Acorns that fell off the tree while their shells were still green are not worth collecting.

◀ All oak trees produce edible acorns that with some effort become nutritious flour and tasty nuts.

PREPARE

There are several different methods for leaching acorns that are described in this section. But whichever method you decide to use, first you need to eliminate any wormy, grub-eaten acorns by putting them to the floater test (these can sneak into your collection even if you were vigilant about inspecting them for holes).

Put your freshly gathered acorns in a big pot or tub of water. The good ones—those heavy with solid nutmeats—will sink to the bottom. The ones that float to the top are light because the nutmeats have already been eaten by grubs or insects, or were rotten and dried out. Discard the floaters. Drain the acorns well, and then either freeze or dry and store them (still in their shells). Note that you may still find some damaged nutmeats when you eventually crack open your non-floaters. You can either discard these, or cut off the undamaged, usable parts.

The next step is to shell the acorns. The thin shells of fresh acorns are quite pliable, making the task of shelling a bit difficult. Although it's possible to use a handheld nutcracker to shell acorns, other methods are more efficient. By far the easiest is to use a piece of equipment specially designed for acorns that has a funnel-shaped opening and a hand crank that moves the nuts through the apparatus: you just dump a quantity of acorns in the funnel section, crank, and they emerge from the bottom with their shells removed or at least thoroughly cracked (see the resources).

Next best is a hammer or a stone. Set the acorn on a board, pavement, or a flat stone, pointy end down (cup end up, but cup removed). Tap sharply one to three times, and the acorn shell will crack neatly along a vertical line making it easy to access the nutmeats inside. Usually the nutmeats will come out in two halves.

Now that the acorns are shelled, you'll notice a thin, reddish brown skin on the nutmeats. Sometimes this comes off easily (freezing the nuts before shelling helps). Other times fragments will cling stubbornly to the nutritious nutmeat. This skin-like layer, which is called a testa, adds a lot of the tannin content to the acorn. But I don't bother spending too much time removing testas because the next step in preparing the acorns takes care of those tannins.

Leaching Acorns

Now you've got to remove the tannins and phytic acid that not only taste awful but also block your body's ability to absorb the excellent nutrients in the acorns

A DaveBuilt Acorn Machine makes processing acorns much easier.

(and other foods you eat with the acorns). To do this, you need to leach them out with water, using one of the two cold water methods or the hot water method, explained below.

The Quickest Cold Water Method

The quickest method for leaching acorns can be completed in 10 minutes or so. However, it has two disadvantages: a lot of the acorn starch that makes for a higher-quality flour gets lost in the process, and it requires an amount of water that isn't practical for arid regions including California and the Southwest. But it does get you from shelled acorns to nutty, mild acorn flour in a remarkably short amount of time.

For this method, put a cup of shelled acorns in a blender and process for 2 to 3 minutes. Drain the acorns into a colander lined with butter muslin (or a clean piece of old sheet). The muslin will catch some, but not all, of the precious acorn starch. Place the acorn meal under a faucet with cold water running for 8 minutes, stirring often. Taste a pinch of the meal. If it is at all bitter, turn the faucet back on and keep stirring. Test again after another 4 minutes. It's ready when you can no longer taste any bitterness or astringency. Wrap the cloth tightly around the acorn meal and squeeze to remove as much moisture as possible. Continue to the finishing steps for cold water leaching, below.

The Slower Cold Water Method

This is by far my favorite way to process acorns. The resulting flour has a higher percentage of the acorn oil and starch than other methods deliver, and although it takes time, very little of it is active time. It uses less water and fuel than the other methods. All you need is patience.

Put a cup of shelled acorns into a blender and fill the blender with water. Blend for 2 minutes. Pour the slurry into a jar or bowl. Alternatively, run the acorn nutmeats through a corn or other grain grinder, or do it the old-fashioned way and pound and roll out the acorns with a stone or wood mortar and pestle or metate. Put the resulting meal in a container, add water, and stir. The amount of water needn't be precise, but the more parts water per part of acorn meal, the faster you'll get the no-longer-tannic result you are after.

The slurry will separate into three layers, with the meal on the bottom, a whitish layer of the valuable starch in the middle, and the tannin-infused water on top. At least once a day, pour off as much of the water as you can without losing too much of the starch (stop when the light-colored starch is starting to pour off, cloud-like, with the water). Add more water, stir vigorously, and let settle. Repeat until the leaching process is complete (see finishing steps below for how to know when it's complete). If you are only going to change the water once a day, store the slurry in the refrigerator. Otherwise, changing the water two or more times daily will be enough to avoid spoilage.

How long will it take to leach your acorns? That depends on the original tannin content of your acorns and how often you change the water. But figure somewhere between 2 and 7 days.

Notice the lighter-colored layer of starch in between the top layer of liquid and the acorn meal on the bottom.

Finishing Steps for Cold Water Leaching

No matter how many times you change the water in the slow method, or how many minutes you let the faucet run in the quick method, the water draining off will never be completely clear. So how do you know when you've done enough leaching? The only sure method is a taste test.

Use a small spoon or your clean fingers to scoop up a small amount of the meal (if you used the slow method, don't drain off the liquid first—I'll explain why in a moment), and taste. If any hint of bitterness remains, it needs more leaching. Even after the flavor is completely mild, you need to check for astringency. If chewing the acorn meal creates even a little bit of a puckering or mouth-drying sensation, it needs more leaching.

Here's why you shouldn't pour the water off the slow-method leached acorns: that liquid contains some of the valuable starch that you want to capture as much of as possible. Once the meal tastes bland enough (and I mean that in a good way), strain it through a fine-mesh sieve over a bowl. Leave the liquid in the bowl to settle for an hour or two. A layer of paste-like, off-white starch will accumulate on the bottom. Pour off the liquid on top and scoop out the gluey starch. You can save the starch to use on its own as a thickener, but I recommend adding it to the strained-off acorn meal. You'll end up with a much higher-quality acorn flour.

The Hot Water Method

With this method, don't bother grinding the acorns before you start leaching them. Instead, boil the freshly shelled acorn nutmeats until the water turns dark brown. Drain, add fresh water, repeat. (You don't have to do hot water leaching all in one day. It's fine to leave the acorns soaking in the water, off the fire, while you go to work, then give them fresh water and bring them back to a boil when you get home.) Keep repeating until a nibble on an acorn confirms that it is neither bitter nor astringent. After this, you can freeze the leached acorns, roast them for a tasty snack, or dry and grind them into flour.

Note that hot water–processed acorn flour has lost all of the starch that enables acorn flour processed via cold water to hold together almost as if it contained gluten. Hot-processed acorn flour is still nutritious and tasty, but it should be combined with other flours in recipes, and even then expect a crumbly texture.

Making Acorn Flour

After grinding and leaching your acorns, you'll have a wet meal that is somewhere between the gritty consistency of cornmeal and fine sand. You need to decide whether to dry your acorn meal so that you can grind it into a finer flour, or pack the still-damp flour into freezer bags or containers and freeze.

Without drying and regrinding, you can still use your acorn meal in combination with other flour to make muffins and quick breads, or on its own to make a very tasty "polenta" (a.k.a. acorn mush). But if you want to make 100 percent acorn bread, pancakes, or anything else with a finer texture, you'll need to dry it and do a second grinding. Keep in mind that acorn flour does not contain gluten. But if it was cold water-processed and most of the acorn starch was preserved, it will stick to itself in a way that results in pleasantly spongy baked and pan-fried foods (acorn blinis are divine!).

To make finely ground acorn flour, spread the acorn meal no more than ¼-inch thick on baking sheets or dehydrator trays. If using a dehydrator, use a low setting such as 95°F. Or turn your oven on to its lowest setting (typically around 150°F), and then prop the door open with a wooden spoon. Or put the tray near a woodstove or fireplace. Dry, stirring occasionally, until no hint of moisture remains. This will take approximately 30 minutes. Regrind in an electric coffee grinder or food processor. Or do it the old-fashioned way and crush the meal between two stones.

A helpful tip to remember is that adding some ground flax or chia seeds to recipes that include a high percentage of acorn flour improves the texture.

PRESERVE

Already ground, leached acorn meal or flour turns rancid if stored at room temperature for more than a month or two. It will keep in the freezer or refrigerator for up to 2 years. I prefer to store most of my acorns whole, still in their shells, and then grind and leach small batches of acorn flour. When I do this, I prepare double the amount of acorn flour I need for a recipe and freeze the excess for the next recipe. That way I always have some on hand.

SWEET LEGUME PODS

With edible legume pods—from lightly sweet honey locust, black locust, and mesquite pods, to chocolaty carob pods—the sweetness is in the pods surrounding the seeds, not the seeds themselves. Edible legume pods can be found all over the United States, with honey locust in areas with cold winters, and the others in the South and Southwest.

The seeds (or beans) of the trees in the legume family are usually too hard and flavorless to be worth eating. Although they have a history of being used as food, I don't think you should waste precious time on them. Carob seeds, for example, will emerge from an electric coffee grinder unscathed. And I once boiled honey locust beans for 12 hours and they *still* weren't tender!

The pods are another story. Once fully ripe (you'll know they are ready to **harvest** when they will start falling from the trees), you can chew on them as is for their sweet taste (spitting out the tough seeds). Or you can **prepare** them by grinding them into a powder. The powder is versatile and can be used to

Honey locust pods are almost as sweet as carob pods when harvested at the right time and prepared correctly.

flavor and enrich homemade energy bars, baked goods, pancakes, breakfast porridges, and even beverages. Because the pods—and the resulting powder—are naturally sweet, you can often get away with using less sugar or other sweeteners than you would if you were using more conventional ingredients. Once prepared, sweet pods are well-**preserved** for months or even years (I just discovered a forgotten stash of 3-year-old homemade carob powder, and it was still wonderfully aromatic and sweet).

CAROB (*Ceratonia siliqua*)

The carob tree is originally from the Mediterranean region and the Middle East, but over the past few centuries humans have introduced it to other continents including North America (California, Southwest and Gulf States including Florida, and Mexico), Portugal, South America, Australia, and South Africa.

FIND AND IDENTIFY

Look for carob anywhere that citrus grows well (in the United States that includes Southern California, Florida, and parts of the Southwest). Not only do the trees appreciate the same sort of climate (hardy down to 20°F but not colder, dry summers, rainy winters), but it was spread by Spanish and British colonists into many of the exact same areas where they introduced citrus. You'll be foraging primarily from feral plants that were once planted intentionally but are now neglected with their sweet harvest going to waste.

Carob is a small to medium-sized broadleaf evergreen tree with alternate, compound leaves. The leaflets are rounded and leathery. The small greenish flowers grow in a spiral arrangement on old wood including spurs on the main scaffold branches of the trees.

The fruits are legume pods that can eventually be up to 10 inches long and as wide as 1 inch across. They take their time maturing: almost a full year from the emergence of the green pods until the dark brown, ripe carobs that drop to the ground in noticeable piles. The hard seeds are used commercially to produce a gum but are not of much practical use to foragers. You're after the sweet, protein-rich pod surrounding the seed.

Carob trees are usually dioecious, meaning that the male and female flowers are produced on separate plants. Only the female plants will produce the seed-bearing pods.

HARVEST

Carob, honey locust, and mesquite pods (including screwbean mesquite) are ready to harvest once fully brown and falling from the tree on their own. You can gather them from the ground, or lay a tarp down and shake the branches. Pods that cling to the branch even when you shake it are not fully ripe yet, and the flavor of those pods won't live up to their sweet potential. They may even be unpleasantly astringent at that stage. If you gather pods that have already fallen to the ground, be sure to give them a thorough rinse before proceeding to the next steps.

The fuzzy, caterpillar-like flowers of the carob tree appear almost a year before the pods are ready to eat.

Often compared to chocolate, carob pods actually have a unique flavor that deserves to be appreciated for its own sake.

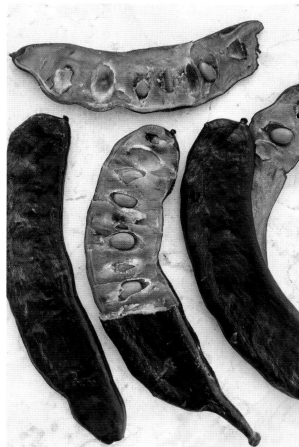

Discard carob's hard seeds; the pods surrounding the seeds are the sweet ingredient you're after.

PREPARE

To prepare, first boil and soak. Put clean pods in a large pot and cover with water. Bring to a boil, then remove from the heat and soak for 12 to 24 hours. This softens the pods and makes it easier to remove the seeds.

Use a paring knife to split the softened pods lengthwise. Remove and discard the seeds. Break the remaining pods into pieces about 1 inch long. Go ahead and nibble on a few while you're working: they are super tasty and will give you energy to complete the task of processing them!

Dry the pod pieces until they are brittle enough to snap in two easily. You can do this in a dehydrator (use a setting between 135°F and 150°F), or in a 200°F oven. This will take 1 to 2 hours. While the pods are drying, your home will smell of something distractingly and enticingly sweet. Once completely dry, grind the pods into a powder using an electric coffee grinder, or, if you want to keep it old school, a flatish stone for a mortar and a round stone for a pestle.

Coarsely ground powder is a useful addition to baked goods, granola, and energy balls or bars. For a finer powder that you can use for hot beverages, custards, and syrups, sift through a fine-mesh sieve. Keep in mind that the powder won't actually dissolve in hot liquid the way chocolate does. But once sifted it will blend into your liquid ingredients quite well.

PRESERVE

By the time they are ripe enough to fall from the tree, carob pods (and other legume pods) are already dry and can be stored at room temperature for weeks without further treatment. Put them in a cloth or paper bag or a basket, and store somewhere with good air circulation. A fellow forager says that he experienced pods losing sweetness in storage. I have not had this experience with carob or other sweet pods, but perhaps it is worth grinding and processing them into powder and keeping the powder in a freezer if you will be storing the carob for longer than a few weeks.

The powder will also keep for months tightly covered in glass or ceramic containers. Plastic will eventually give the powder an off taste, so I don't recommend it.

GINKGO (*Ginkgo biloba*)

What has a shell and is at the center of a pulpy, soft-skinned fruit, yet is neither a pit nor a seed? Introducing ginkgo, a rule breaker that foragers almost universally refer to as a "nut" even though we know better.

Ginkgo trees evolved 150 million years ago before any flowering plants, and technically all seeds including nuts come from flowers, so ginkgo cannot have true seeds (the ginkgo's nut is actually a gametophyte). The nut is surrounded by juicy orange pulp, but you don't want to eat that. Not only does the pulp stink like vomit (sorry, but that's accurate), it can cause an allergic reaction on some people's skin. The nut, however, is delicious and a prized ingredient in the Far East and with foragers wherever it grows.

Ginkgo's smelly orange pulp hides a pistachio-green treat inside a thin shell.

FIND AND IDENTIFY

Both male and female ginkgo trees have fan-shaped leaves with roughly parallel veins that run all the way to the edge of the leaf. There is usually a notch or two in the wide end of the fan. The leaves turn bright yellow and fall to the ground in autumn.

Because of their attractive foliage and high tolerance of both pollution and cold winter temperatures, ginkgos are frequently planted as street trees and in city parks. They are also extremely long lived (some ginkgo trees are close to 3,000 years old). But trust me, no city planner ever actually means to plant female ginkgo trees. It's just that the male and females are difficult to tell apart (except when the females are in fruit), so numerous female ginkgos have been unintentionally planted in urban landscapes.

Both male and female ginkgo trees can grow to be 70 feet tall. The bark on young trees and branches is smooth, but mature trees have deep, rough furrows. The orange fruits are about the size of a Ping-Pong ball and start falling to the ground in October or November in most locations. Inside the smelly pulp is a smooth, cream-colored shell. Inside that is a soft, pistachio-green nut encased in a papery brown membrane.

HARVEST

I discovered my favorite harvesting method for ginkgo nuts when I went for a winter walk and found some still on the ground where they had fallen from the tree. This was in January after many freezes and thaws. The shells were perfectly cleaned with no trace of the putrid pulp remaining. However, that is a rare find.

Typically, you will follow your nose to the orange fruit piling up beneath the tree in October or November. Wear plastic gloves (or in a pinch, put your hands inside plastic bags) to prevent the nasty skin rash that ginkgo pulp juice gives some people. I like to field dress the nuts by squishing off the pulp and skins and leaving them behind. If you can find a nearby water fountain, go ahead and wash the still-in-their-shells nuts before bringing them home.

PREPARE

Ginkgo nuts must be cooked to be edible. Spread washed ginkgo nuts, still in their shells, in a single layer on baking sheets. Bake at 300°F for 30 minutes.

The edible part of ginkgo is the green seed (technically a gametophyte) hidden within the stinky orange pulp.

To eat, remove the thin shells from the roasted nuts. I like to use a small hammer to lightly crack the shells and then remove them. You could use a handheld nutcracker, but it is hard to avoid smashing the soft nut inside. Try to remove as much of the brown membrane between the shell and the soft nut as possible, but don't worry if a few fragments remain.

Once roasted and shelled, you can see the beautiful pistachio-green color and enjoy the texture, which is similar to a cooked bean. They are good as a snack lightly salted or tossed with tamari sauce and re-roasted for 5 minutes. They are also intriguing in soups. Puréed into dips and spreads, they have a texture almost like soft cheese.

PRESERVE

The best way to preserve ginkgo nuts is to freeze them already roasted but still in their shells. If you want to freeze them already shelled, I recommend a vacuum sealer because they dry out and become hard even in tightly sealed freezer containers or ziplock bags.

11

BARK AND TWIGS

EATING BARK SOUNDS like something you would only want to do in a desperate survival situation. But surprisingly, the inner bark of trees including birch, basswood, sassafras, and pine can be both nutritious and tasty. It is also a wild food that you can forage at any time of year, even in regions with harsh winters.

Bark has a long history of being used as food. Adirondack, the name of a part of New York State, means "bark eater." It was the name given by the Mohawks to the Algonquins who lived in that region. The Nez Perce also used bark, not only as survival food but as a food of choice. And bark is a traditional food of many Scandinavian cultures.

Think bark and twigs aren't food? Think again.

EDIBLE BARK

Before we get down to the nitty-gritty of how to eat bark in ways that are (1) sustainable (the harvest doesn't kill the tree), and (2) tasty (not just edible), let's define bark. With rare exceptions, edible bark is not the scruffy stuff on the outside of the tree trunk or branch. Instead, foragers are after the inner bark.

It is important to understand why this part of the tree is edible, and why incorrectly harvesting it could kill the tree. The layer we call the inner bark is just under the rough outer bark. This inner bark includes the phloem, cambium, and outer secondary xylem (sapwood). These tissues combine in a layer that is soft, lightly sweet, and more nutrient-dense and digestible than the outer bark or the heartwood. Why? This is the layer that contains the transport tissues through which much of the water and minerals comes up from the roots, and where the sugars produced by photosynthesis travel down from the

▶ Silvery-white with striking black horizontal marks, birch bark is easy to identify at any time of year.

It is illegal to strip bark from trees in national forests even if you are using the sustainable techniques in this chapter.

leaves to the rest of the plant. The cambium layer is a region of active growth that produces xylem and phloem, as well as cork. This combination of water, nutrients, and sugar transport plus a meristematic (active growth) region makes the inner bark layer moist and flavorful.

Once you understand that the inner bark is the transport zone for water, nutrients, and carbohydrates in a tree, it becomes obvious why "girdling" the tree can kill it. Girdling is cutting off a strip of bark *around the entire circumference of the trunk*. Think about it: Let's say you've removed a strip of bark all around the trunk of the tree. Some of the water coming up from the roots hits that cut and can't make it up to the branches and leaves. The leaves are busy photosynthesizing, but when the sugar they are creating tries to travel down to the roots, it hits your girdling slash in the bark and can't go any farther. The gap in the transport zone kills the tree. Another issue is the risk of disease and infestation. A big, gaping hole in the bark can invite fungal infections and bug problems.

If you want to **harvest** inner bark without killing the tree, you must ensure that there is plenty of intact cambium, phloem, and sapwood around the trunk to enable that transport up from the roots and down from the leaves. I explain several ways to do so in the harvest section of the pine plant profile on page 193 (the methods apply to all trees with edible inner bark).

I've found two ways to use bark that are worth the effort of **preparing** them: dried and then ground into flour, and fried in very thin strips. Some people reportedly tear the inner bark into strips and boil them like spaghetti, but I've tried this several times and the result was chewy and unpleasant. Don't bother.

You can **preserve** bark simply by drying it. However, delicately aromatic barks such as birch and sassafras lose most of their flavor after more than 6 months in storage.

PINE (*Pinus* species)

FIND AND IDENTIFY

The *Pinus* genus contains over a hundred species, and all of them are aromatic, evergreen, and resinous, with bundles of long, linear leaves commonly called needles. The number of needles per bundle is one of the ways to distinguish different species within the genus. These needles stay in groups of two to five and are held together at the base with a papery sheath.

Long (1½ inches or usually longer) needles are a hallmark of this genus. Other evergreen conifers with shorter, needle-like leaves may or may not be edible. For example, young spruce's (*Picea*) short needles are an excellent wild edible, whereas yew's (*Taxus*) needles (and bark) are toxic. With pine, the needles are long and round rather than flat.

Pine trees and shrubs produce two types of cones of woody, scale-like pieces around a central core. One type produces pollen, and the other may eventually house an edible pine "nut" under each scale. Pine trees are frequently conical in shape (the classic Christmas tree), but depending on habitat and age may be flat-topped and wind bent. The best pine nut–producing species have branches that grow in an umbrella shape.

HARVEST

Windfall

The most surefire way not to hurt the tree is to keep an eye out for freshly fallen branches after a storm. Once separated from the tree, the inner bark dries out quickly and is no longer good to eat. But if you find some freshly fallen branches within 2 to 3 weeks after a storm, go for it.

Come in at an angle with a pocket knife and work down the branch in strips. You'll be able to feel the harder wood layer below the inner bark. Strip off the layer just outside that. You'll be getting the dry outer bark as well, but you can peel or rub that off later.

Prune a Branch

Another option is to prune a branch from the tree or shrub and then strip the inner bark from the branch. Correct pruning methods should be used to minimize disease potential, most importantly cutting just past the branch collar

Pine trees provide at least three and sometimes four edible parts, including the inner bark.

(the slightly wider area where the branch attaches to the tree). The branch collar contains special tissues that rapidly heal the cut, but it can't do its job if you cut off the branch flush with the trunk.

The Narrow Vertical Cut

The last method is to make a narrow, vertical cut on the main trunk. Indigenous peoples on more than one continent have frequently used this method. And although many arborists would advise against it, there *is* a way to do this without causing any permanent damage to the tree.

Use a knife to score a vertical rectangle in the bark. The rectangle should be no wider than 1 inch. It is important to keep it small because the wider the wound, the longer it will take the tree to heal. Making the strip vertical rather than horizontal minimizes interruption of the tree's food and water transport zones.

A narrow vertical cut minimizes damage to the tree while allowing the harvest of strips of tender inner bark.

Keep scratching across the four sides of the rectangle in a tic-tac-toe-like pattern until you hit the harder wood beneath the bark. Slip the edge of your knife between the soft inner bark layer and the wood, and pull the inner bark off in strips.

It is much easier to use this method on young trees with relatively thin outer bark. Not only is working with young trees easier on your foraging knife, but such trees recover more quickly, in my experience. The inner bark of young trees will also be less resinous than mature trees.

Note: You should not use this method in regions where Dutch elm disease, butternut canker, mountain pine beetle, emerald ash borers, or other tree diseases or infestations are a problem. If you're not sure if these problems apply to your area, contact your county extension office.

OTHER EDIBLE PARTS OF PINE

Of the many species of pine, only a few produce seeds or "nuts" that are big enough to be worth harvesting. These species (including *Pinus pinea* and *P. monophylla*) mostly grow around the Mediterranean, in the North American West, and in the Middle East but have been introduced as permaculture plantings in a few other regions.

Though delicious, pine nuts are labor intensive to harvest and shell (hence the high price of commercial pine nuts). If you are lucky enough to live near one of the species worth harvesting, you'll know they are ready to gather in summer and early fall when you notice the black, torpedo-shaped shells on the ground. The cream-colored kernel we are familiar with is inside the black, speckled shell.

The new, light green growth tips of all pine species are an interesting flavoring ingredient. Mince and add as a seasoning to a wide variety of foods from salmon to sorbet. The green pine cones have been used for their high wild yeast content to start fermentations from sourdough to booze. Be quick about getting the green, still-closed pinecones from tree to ferment: stored for even a few days, they lose their power to kick-start fermentation.

PREPARE

To make pine bark "bacon," use only thin strips of fresh, moist pine inner bark. Remove the outer bark and any green, resinous parts. Heat a lipid of your choice—oil, butter, or animal fat—in a skillet over medium-high heat. Use just enough oil or fat to coat the pan.

Fry the pine bark strips on each side until they turn reddish brown, about 1 to 2 minutes per side. Remove from the pan and sprinkle with salt while still hot. You can play with the seasonings: I like a little ground chipotle for smoky flavor. You can also cook them in a pan over a campfire and get a naturally smoky taste that way.

Hot from the pan, the texture will be slightly crunchy and slightly chewy with a hint of sweetness, very much like bacon. Once cooled and stored for a few hours, you'll have more crunch than chew, but that's not necessarily a bad thing.

Fried pine bark is crisp but not dry, with hints of sweetness and barely noticeable but pleasant evergreen.

PRESERVE

Preserve the refreshing taste and aroma of young pine growth by infusing spring pine branch tips in vinegar, and use in dressings and marinades. For the tender new growth needles, finely mince and mix with sugar or salt to create a condiment that can be sprinkled over other ingredients. Use a ratio of 4 parts minced young pine needles to 1 part either sugar or salt.

Pine nuts turn rancid rapidly if stored at room temperature. Store them in the freezer, refrigerator, or other cool place.

The inner bark of pine is best used fresh as in the pine bark bacon recipe. Once fried, pine bark bacon will keep in sealed containers at room temperature for several weeks.

TREES WITH THE TASTIEST EDIBLE BARK

Of the edible barks I've sampled so far, these are my favorites. Where I haven't named a particular species, all species within that genus have bark that is edible and safe to eat. I have no doubt that numerous other safe and tasty edible barks are out there. Let me know if you have experience with any not on my short, personal "tastiest" list.

Birch (*Betula*)
Basswood/Linden (*Tilia*)
Maple (*Acer*)

Pine (*Pinus*)
Sassafras (*Sassafras albidum*)
Slippery Elm (*Ulmus rubra*)

WARNING Not all woody plants have edible bark. Some may have other edible parts but inedible bark. For example, some may have edible flowers (e.g., *Wisteria*), or edible flowers and fruit (e.g., elderberry, *Sambucus*), but all other parts of the plant are poisonous. Yew (*Taxus*) has red arils with edible pulp, but the rest of the tree or shrub is poisonous. Remember the first rule of foraging: if in doubt, leave it out.

RULE BREAKER

SHAGBARK HICKORY (*Carya ovata*)

It is almost always the inner bark of trees that we use for food, but an exception is shagbark hickory. Its craggy outer bark, which peels off the tree easily, is popular among foragers as a syrup flavoring. Infused in syrup, it gives a wonderful nutty, caramel flavor.

FIND AND IDENTIFY

Look for shagbark hickory (and other hickories) in open woods and at the edges of fields. Shagbark hickory trees can get as tall as 110 feet. They are easily identified because of their rough grayish outer bark that peels off the tree in long strips.

Like other hickories, *Carya ovata* has alternate, compound leaves up to a foot long with an odd number of leaflets with serrated edges (most often five or seven leaflets per compound leaf). In spring, hickory's separate male and female catkins dangle from the branches. The male catkins are longer than the female ones. The nuts are not quite round and covered in a hard, four-ribbed shell. Both nut and shell are further encased in a thick husk that turns from green to brown as the nuts ripen.

All hickory trees begin with smooth gray bark that develops craggy vertical ridges as the trees get older. In the case of the shagbark hickory, those vertical ridges partially detach, giving the bark its name-worthy shaggy appearance.

HARVEST

You are not diving down into the inner bark, so don't worry about girdling the tree. Just look for already partially detached strips of outer bark and peel them off. The nuts drop from the trees in late summer and early fall. Use one of the methods for hard-shelled nuts on page 163.

PREPARE

The bark of a mature shagbark hickory can be used as syrup flavoring at any time. Use a vegetable brush and either running water from a faucet or a bucket of water to scrub your bark pieces clean (do not let the bark sit in the water for more than a few minutes). Then spread the bark pieces on a baking sheet (or a rack at the outer, cooler edges of campfire coals). Bake at 350°F for 30 minutes.

OTHER USES FOR EDIBLE BARK

Birch bark makes a lovely infusion (black and yellow birches especially, because of their wintergreen flavor). Ground into a flour, it adds delightful flavor to baked goods such as shortbread.

Slippery elm bark has a mucilaginous texture when cooked in water, which means you can boil it into a thick porridge. It has a lovely maple-like flavor and a reputation as being good for recovering from extended illnesses, as well as soothing sore throats, coughs, and tummy troubles. Cherry bark is prized as a cough remedy (the original cherry cough drops had nothing to do with the sweet fruit but were based on the effectiveness of the bark). Another inner bark with medicinal properties is willow. It contains salicin, which the body converts into salicylic acid, an anti-inflammatory and pain-relieving precursor for aspirin.

One use for edible inner bark that I advise against is bark as pasta. The idea is that you take skinny strips of cambium, boil them, and then add a sauce. I've tried this several times, and have yet to arrive at a texture I found palatable. If you manage to pull it off, let me know your secret.

Transfer the bark to a pot and barely cover with water. Bring to a boil, reduce heat, and simmer for 30 minutes. Strain out the shagbark hickory bark, reserving the liquid. Measure the liquid and add an equal amount of sugar or maple syrup. Simmer until the liquid is reduced by half.

PRESERVE

Process pint canning jars of shagbark hickory syrup in a boiling water bath for 10 minutes. Once canned and sealed, the syrup will keep indefinitely. The dried, intact bark will still have good flavor after 3 years if stored in airtight containers away from direct light or heat.

◄ There's a reason it is called shagbark. Enough said.

TWIGS

Think twigs don't sound tasty? Think again. While they may never be the main course on your plate, they can certainly enhance your food with flavor. You've probably eaten "cedar-planked" or "hickory-smoked" food. Those are examples of woody tree parts flavoring our food in good ways. But twigs are better because they are the active growth tips of tree branches, more aromatic and flavorful than the woody stuff back toward the trunk.

Trees and shrubs with aromatic and tasty twigs include sassafras, birch, spicebush, basswood, and others.

Usually sought after for its aromatic fruits, spicebush also has flavorful twigs and leaves.

SASSAFRAS (*Sassafras albidum*)

FIND AND IDENTIFY

Sassafras trees grow in the woodlands of eastern North America and are also planted by landscapers in urban parks. They can grow up to 50 feet tall and, when mature, the bark is rough and reddish brown, but the bark of young twigs at the end of the branches is green. It is common for there to be many suckers coming up from the roots of the trees, often giving the appearance of a sassafras shrub growing at the base of the parent tree (novice foragers may miss the fact that it is the same tree).

The key identification characteristic for sassafras is three different leaf shapes on one tree: a simple oval, a three-lobed shape, and a two-lobed mitten shape. The leaves grow in an alternate arrangement (they join the twigs singly rather than in pairs). Another tree that (depending on species) may have these same three leaf shapes is mulberry. But mulberry leaves are toothed, whereas sassafras leaves have smooth margins. In autumn, sassafras leaves turn yellow, orange, or red before they fall to the forest floor.

Every part of sassafras is aromatic, and this should also be part of your ID. The roots give off a strong root beer smell (it's not that sassafras smells like root beer, but rather that root beer was originally made with sassafras). The fragrance of the twigs, bark, and leaves is milder with citrusy notes that the roots lack.

HARVEST

Sassafras leaves are at their best in mid-spring, but you can harvest them any time they are green. The twigs and roots can be harvested anytime. When harvesting the twigs, simply snap off the outer few inches of a branch: the tree will recover from that without trouble. To harvest sassafras roots, I like to look for young saplings under 3 feet tall growing under the mature trees. It is easy to pull these up, especially if a recent rain has softened the soil. Do not attempt to harvest the large roots of mature trees by hacking away at them, as this could harm the tree.

PREPARE

My favorite way to use the twigs is to first break them into small pieces and put in a pot. Barely cover with water, and bring to a boil. Remove from the heat, and then cover the pot and let steep for 30 to 60 minutes (longer steeping

Easily identifiable by the smooth-margined leaves in three shapes on one tree (oval, three-lobed, and mitten shape), sassafras bark smells and tastes like a wonderful combination of root beer and citrus.

results in a more bitter extraction). Strain, and use to create your own sodas (add a little sweetener and seltzer), cocktails, and sauces. You can do the same with sassafras roots, with a much stronger, more root beer-y result.

If you like Creole gumbo, then you may know that one of the ingredients is something called filé powder, which is dried, powdered sassafras leaves. I make mine by hanging up harvested branch tips for a few days, then powdering the leaves in an electric coffee grinder.

PRESERVE

The twigs store well in cloth or paper bags or baskets (something with air circulation) for up to 6 months. But my favorite way to preserve sassafras twigs is to simmer them in just enough water to cover for 10 minutes, let steep (covered) for another 10 minutes, then strain and add an equal amount of sugar or honey. This is a lighter version of the extraction method above. Use this delightful syrup in homemade sodas and cocktails. Give it as a gift to the mixologist in your life.

The roots keep well, dried, in containers that have some air flow. Store dried sassafras leaves crumbled or whole, then grind them just before you use them in gumbo.

12

SAP

Maple (*Acer* species)   206

TIMING IS EVERYTHING when it comes to tapping trees for their sweet sap, and that timing varies depending on the type of tree. With maple, the sap run occurs when it's warmer than freezing during the day but still freezing at night, usually between mid-February and mid-March. Once the trees start to leaf out, sugaring season is over. Birch, basswood, walnut, and other tappable trees have their sugaring season just after the maple sap run ends.

WARNING Only tap trees with a trunk diameter of more than 12 inches. If the diameter of the tree is less than 20 inches, never drill more than one tap hole. If the trunk diameter is 20 to 27 inches, you can drill two tap holes; over 27 inches, three tap holes. Too many tap holes for the size of the tree could damage it.

MAPLE (*Acer* species)

Maple is the most famous of the sugaring trees because it gives you more syrup per gallon of sap than other trees. For example, a typically cited ratio (although in my experience this varies from year to year) is 40:1 for sugar maple (*Acer saccharum*), black maple (*A. nigrum*), red maple (*A. rubrum*), and silver maple (*A. saccharinum*). That means that it can take 40 gallons of sap to get 1 gallon of syrup. With other *Acer* species, the ratio may be as much as 80:1. By comparison, it can take as much as 100 gallons of birch sap to produce 1 gallon of syrup. That is why you're more likely to find maple than birch syrup on your supermarket shelf.

FIND AND IDENTIFY

Maple trees are shade tolerant and frequently grow in mixed hardwood forests. Famous for their brilliantly colorful fall foliage, maple trees, which can live for over 200 years, can get huge: up to 100 feet high and 2½ feet in trunk diameter. Maple trees need to be 40 to 60 years old before they can be tapped.

Maple leaves have three- or five-pointed lobes (*Acer*, the genus name, means sharp). They are arranged alternately (joining the branches in pairs) and are between 2 and 7 inches across. Although you may already be familiar with the shape of maple leaves (it's the symbol on the Canadian flag), it is important to learn to identify maple trees in winter when they lack leaves. Late winter is sugaring season—the time to collect the sweet sap. Of course, one way is to identify and stake out the trees while they still have leaves during the growing season or autumn.

With or without leaves, maple trees have leaf buds in pairs almost surrounded by V-shaped leaf scars with three marks (bundle scars) that look a bit like a face emoji. Single, longer buds appear on the ends of the twigs. You'll also probably see some of the samaras (winged seeds) that dropped in late autumn lying on the ground under the tree. The bark of maple trees is smooth when young. But on trees old enough to tap, the gray to almost black bark will be deeply furrowed and in rough strips.

HARVEST

There are two methods for tapping a tree for sap. One can be done with little more equipment than a twig, the other is closer to how it is done commercially.

Say "pancake syrup," and most North Americans immediately think of maple syrup. It's not just because maple provides more syrup per gallon of sap than other trees but also its unique flavor that seasons any recipe as much as it sweetens it.

A simple spile releases the flow of sweet sap. Maple is not the only syrup that is fantastic drizzled on your pancakes. Other trees including black walnut, birch, and linden can also provide both sweetness and great flavor that is concentrated when the sap gets boiled down to syrup.

OTHER FOOD FROM MAPLE TREES

Maple trees provide two other foods that are worth mentioning. The immature samaras or winged seeds are edible. Gather these when the seed end is round and plump but the "wing" is still entirely green. Break off the wing and squeeze out the seed. You can dry or roast these as is, but I prefer to blanch them for 5 minutes in boiling water first to remove bitterness. Newly unfurled maple leaves are also edible. See the section on edible tree leaves on page 57 for tips on when and how to harvest them.

For the first method, carve one end of a twig to a sharp, flat point. Place the sharpened end against the trunk at an upward angle. Tap the twig into the trunk with a rock, hammer, or knife handle. Sap will flow out of the tree and along the twig. If it runs down the tree's bark instead of along the twig, carve a narrow groove along the length of the twig. Place a plastic bottle or a lightweight bucket directly under the twig (which is now acting as a spile). Secure the container to the tree by tying around it and the tree with string or duct tape. The twig spile will transport a slow drip of sap. Check your bottles and pails every day, and you'll eventually have enough sap for a small batch of homemade syrup.

For the other method, drill at a slight angle upward using a $\frac{7}{16}$- or $\frac{5}{16}$-inch bit. Go in about 2 inches deep. Insert a metal spile (see the resources) into the hole. Use a hammer or rock to tap it securely into place. Then attach plastic tubing and let the sap flow down into a bucket on the ground, or attach a hook to the spile and hang a bucket from the hook.

PREPARE

Filter the sap through cheesecloth or a fine-mesh sieve to remove debris. You can stockpile your filtered sap in the refrigerator for up to a week.

To turn sap into syrup, boil it in an open pot so that the water content can evaporate and the liquid can concentrate. Don't pour in more than an inch or so of sap at a time—more will result in the heartache of watching your hard-won sap boil over the top of the pot.

MY FAVORITE TREE SAPS

Many trees have sweet, edible sap. Sometimes I skip the boiling down to syrup altogether and just treat the sap as a naturally sweet, lightly aromatic beverage.

Basswood/Linden	Butternut
Birch	Maple
Black Walnut	Sycamore

At first a lot of steam will come off from your boiling sap (this is why this stage is usually done outdoors). Eventually, there will be less steam and you should start testing your syrup for readiness (keep in mind that it will have a thinner texture while hot than after it has cooled).

Keep a plate in the freezer (or simply outside if it's freezing out). Pour a small bit of the syrup onto the plate. If after 30 seconds the syrup's consistency is thick but still pourable, it's done.

PRESERVE

Syrup made by boiling down tree sap will keep in the refrigerator or other cold place for up to 3 months. For longer storage at room temperature, process the syrup in pint canning jars for 10 minutes (longer if you are at a higher than sea level altitude).

13

MUSHROOMS

A GOOD WILD EDIBLE MUSHROOM find can bring a gleam to a forager's eye that few other wild edibles can spark. Hit a motherlode of chicken of the woods and I bet you're posting pics as fast as you can take them. But at the same time, many people are terrified of eating any wild mushroom. That's true even if they occasionally forage wild fruit or vegetables. Obviously, entire books have been written about how to safely identify and prepare wild edible mushrooms. As with the plant sections, I am not trying to share comprehensive field guide

▶ Saffron milkcap, blewit, and granulated slippery jack mushrooms harvested from a pine forest.

knowledge species by species. Instead, I hope to give you some overview skills for mushroom hunting that will serve you for a lifetime.

It's called plant "foraging" but mushroom "hunting" for good reason. Mushrooms can be much more elusive than plants. For example, if I picked an abundance of the perennial edible pokeweed (*Phytolacca americana*) in a certain spot last spring, I can count on finding it there again the following year. But there's no guarantee that the oak tree that sprouted maitake mushroom at its base last fall is going to do so again this year or that I'll get the timing right when I visit "my" chanterelle spot.

Location and seasonal specifics are super important for mushroom identification. Please consult a reliable field guide (see the resources) to help you factor in these details when you are trying to identify a new-to-you mushroom. For example, if you told me that you found oyster mushrooms growing in a lawn I would assume that either you misidentified the mushroom or you didn't see a buried stump or log (oyster mushrooms grow on wood). And if you told me you found a morel in November, I would confidently reply that you did not (morels are a spring mushroom).

Many mushrooms are also associated with specific plant species, and that, too, is an important part of identifying them. Saffron milkcap mushrooms (*Lactarius deliciosus*), for example, grow under pine trees. Other important mushroom identification factors include whether or not the mushroom stains a particular color when sliced or bruised; whether it does or does not exude a particular color liquid when the gill layer (if it has one) is nicked; and last but certainly not least, scent. You already know that I am a big fan of scratch-and-sniff foraging when it comes to plants. That is equally true when it comes to mushrooms. Some mushrooms have distinctive aromas that are absolutely a part of their ID. For example, dryad's saddle (*Polyporus squamosus*) really does smell remarkably like watermelon.

As with plants, it is essential to be 100 percent certain of your identification. In addition to physical characteristics such as shape and color, take note of where (in leaf litter? on wood?) and what time of year the mushroom was growing. It is worth taking a spore print (see page 226) to confirm your visual ID.

Harvest mushrooms, a.k.a. the fruiting body of the fungal organism, at soil level, leaving the mycelium (what some people mistakenly refer to as the "roots" of the mushroom) behind in the earth. Do not carry fungi in plastic bags or containers because they will become slimy and unappetizing. Instead, use cloth or paper bags or woven baskets to get them home. My mentor Gary

Lincoff recommended rolling up freshly harvested mushrooms in waxed paper twisted at either end to create a container.

Before **preparing** your recipe, give your wild mushrooms a light scrub with a vegetable brush under cold water (ignore that old advice about not using water because the mushrooms will soak it up—it simply isn't true). If the mushrooms are at all buggy, soak them for a few minutes in heavily salted water (about 2 tablespoons of salt per quart of water), then rinse them off before proceeding with your recipe.

Most wild mushrooms are good simply sautéed in butter or oil with a little garlic and salt. Go gentle on the heat. The mushrooms will first release their liquid. Then the liquid will disappear, partly reabsorbed into the mushrooms and partly evaporated. Mushrooms can also be grilled (skewers of marinated mushrooms with other vegetables or meat are classic) or baked (toss with extra-virgin olive oil or another lipid and salt before putting in a single layer in a baking dish).

Slightly old and therefore more porous mushrooms are better puréed in soups, or dehydrated and then reconstituted before cooking. Another trick if the flavor is good but the texture tough, is to first dehydrate and then grind the mushroom. Use the powder to pump up the flavor in mushroom-first dishes such as mushroom risotto.

Note that *all* wild mushrooms should be cooked before they are eaten.

Most mushrooms are best **preserved** by dehydrating. Use a dehydrator to preserve the color, but a low oven temperature works just as well to preserve flavor (expect darkening, though). Use a temperature somewhere between 95°F and 125°F if using a dehydrator. If using an oven, use the lowest setting; if that is 150°F or higher, prop the oven door open with the handle of a wooden spoon. To use dried mushrooms, pour boiling water over them and let them soak for 10 to 20 minutes depending on the thickness of the pieces. Remove the mushrooms from the soaking liquid, squeeze out excess liquid, and proceed with cooking as you would with fresh mushrooms. Don't throw out that soaking liquid! It is loaded with flavor and fantastic in soups, sauces, risotto, and more.

All mushrooms can also be well preserved by first cooking and then freezing them. For example, sauté some chestnut boletes in oil or butter until cooked through, let cool, and then pack into freezer bags or containers and freeze. Densely fleshy, not very spongy mushrooms such as maitake (hen of the woods, *Grifola frondosa*) can be successfully frozen without cooking them first.

Pickling mushrooms is another good way to **preserve** them. Pickled mushrooms are traditionally served with a cold vodka chaser in Russia and eastern Europe. However, a few mushrooms are edible only if they are *not* combined with alcohol, such as the common inky cap (*Coprinopsis atramentaria*). Research which mushrooms this is an issue with before you pour that shot of vodka.

CAP AND STEM MUSHROOMS WITH PORES

Cap and stem mushrooms with pores not gills (such as *Boletus*, *Suillus*, and *Tylopilus*) are considered relatively safe mushrooms compared to cap and stem mushrooms *with* gills (but that doesn't mean you don't need to confirm your ID). From the top or side, mushrooms in this category look much the same as gilled cap and stem mushrooms. But flip one over, and instead of gills on the underside of the cap, you'll find a spongy layer of pores.

Porcini, called cepes in France (*Boletus edulis*), mushrooms are the best known among the choice mushrooms in this category. It is not uncommon to hear all mushrooms in this category referred to as "boletes" even though technically only those in the *Boletus* genus merit that name.

In late summer through fall in Europe, Russia, and other fungi-enthusiastic countries you'll find families out gathering this type of mushroom. The reason is that their pore-not-gill undersides are very easy to recognize, and they are safe enough to taste test. This means that if you've found cap and stem mushrooms with a spongy pore undersurface instead of gills, you can safely nibble a bit. If it is bitter, spit it out. Not only does the bitterness mean that mushroom wouldn't be good eats but also that it could make you sick. Another tip is to avoid those with orange or reddish pore surfaces (although exceptions to this tip do exist).

For detailed individual species **identification**, you'll need a mushroom field guide or reliable website. It is beyond the scope of this book to cover all the individual mushroom species information, but know that you need to think about location (meadow, deep woods, etc.), associated plants (oak, pine, etc.), and season when keying out the mushroom you've found. For example, some cap and stem mushrooms with pores rather than gills only grow near pine trees while others prefer oaks.

So there it is: a round, fleshy mushroom cap. When you **harvest** by slicing or snapping it off at the base of the stipe (the "stem" of the mushroom), you

Unlike supermarket button mushrooms, these *Tylopilus* mushrooms have pores rather than gills on the underside of their caps.

see that the stipe is fairly thick. Most importantly, you'll find a spongy pore layer instead of gills on the underside of the cap. In young mushrooms, this layer may be so dense and firm that it seems almost solid. In older ones it will be more porous, like an old foam kitchen sponge. The pore layer is your major clue as to whether the mushroom, assuming it is an edible species, will be good to eat. The firmer and less soggy the pore layer, the better the texture of your final product.

Among the cap and stem mushrooms with pores, *Boletus* and *Tylopilus* mushrooms are divine simply sautéed and lightly seasoned. *Suillus* mushrooms need more **preparation**: Peel them, using a paring knife to remove the cap skin. I also recommend removing the pore layer from any of the mushrooms in this category if it is more than a centimeter thick (the texture once cooked will be better).

All the mushrooms in this category can be **preserved** by dehydration, and some are even improved by the drying. You can also cook the mushrooms in a little oil or butter and then freeze them.

GRANULATED SLIPPERY JACK/ORANIOT
(*Suillus granulatus*)

I know, I know. Experienced foragers are raising their eyebrows and asking, "Why this one, when there are so many tastier cap and stem, pored-rather-than-gilled mushrooms?" And that's exactly why.

If you've found a king bolete or a comparably choice pored cap and stem mushroom, you don't need any more help from me. Bon appétit. But often the most abundant edible mushrooms are not the sexiest. Knowing how to turn them into something desirable should be one of your foraging skills.

While spending time in Israel, I found that these mushrooms were especially prized. Was that because they were the most abundant and not many other wild edible mushrooms were available? Perhaps. But it's exactly that kind of use-what-you've-got inventiveness that has given us some of the best signature dishes in regions around the world. So I got curious, I asked questions, and I learned how to turn this mushroom—abundant on several continents but often snubbed—into an ingredient worth celebrating.

FIND AND IDENTIFY
Suillus granulatus grows in association with pine trees. Look for it during cool, rainy weather where the pine duff (fallen pine needles) layer is several inches thick. The mushrooms will have pushed the duff up slightly and be barely peeking out.

The caps will be slightly slimy or shiny and almost always have a few pine needles stuck to them. The underside of the caps will have a pore layer that is creamy or light yellow in young mushrooms, becoming mustard yellow-brown in older specimens. Look closely at the stipes and you'll see that they are speckled with dark spots (hence the "granulated" part of the common name). All parts of the mushroom turn bright yellow soon after being cut. The spore print is brown.

HARVEST
Use a pocket knife to slice the slippery jacks off just above soil level.

PREPARE
Use a paring knife to peel off the slightly slimy cap skins. This step is not optional: leave the caps unpeeled and some of your dinner guests will have

This mushroom can be abundant in pine forests (it is always associated with pine). Often disparaged by foragers, it can be fantastic when prepared correctly.

diarrhea. I also peel away the pore layer on the underside of the caps, but this is optional.

Suillus mushrooms are not good candidates for simple pan frying. But they are excellent cooked with chicken or vegetable broth and then turned into a puréed soup. Or dry them first, after which their texture is much better when pan fried. Or dry and then powder them in an electric grinder and use the powder to add umami flavor and thicken sauces, soups, and grain dishes. You can also use fresh, minced *Suillus* mushrooms instead of egg as the glue to hold together veggie burgers.

PRESERVE

Once you've removed the cap skin and pore layers, slice the mushrooms no thicker than ½ inch and dehydrate them until brittle. To rehydrate, simply pour boiling water over them and let them soak for 15 minutes. Drain, squeeze out as much water as you can, and proceed to sauté or otherwise cook as you would fresh mushrooms.

MUSHROOMS WITHOUT STEMS OR GILLS

Wild edible mushrooms in this category include some of the easiest to identify and the choicest gourmet fungi. What's not to love? Note that foragers frequently use the words *stipe* and *stem* interchangeably. Whatever you call it, these mushrooms don't have one.

To **harvest** these mushrooms, use a sharp knife to slice off the mushroom just outside its attachment (usually to bark or wood).

Preparing pored, stipeless mushrooms is as simple as sautéing them in the lipid of your choice and then using the cooked mushrooms in risotto, pasta, omelets, or gravy. Or better yet, just dig in with a fork and call it dinner.

All mushrooms in this category can be **preserved** by first cooking then freezing. The ones with very solid, dense flesh such as maitake and chicken of the woods can be frozen without cooking first. Drying is a second-best option.

Hen of the woods, also called maitake (*Grifola frondosa*), is one of the easiest to identify and most delicious wild mushrooms. It has neither stems nor gills.

CHICKEN OF THE WOODS (*Laetiporus* species)

FIND AND IDENTIFY

Chicken of the woods is a shelf mushroom with pores, not gills, on the underside. Its upper surface will be bright orange or yellow, or occasionally mostly white. The easiest to spot "chicken," *Laetiporus sulphureus*, grows on oak and other hardwoods in the eastern half of North America. On the West Coast, *L. gilbertsonii* grows on both oak and eucalyptus. But in any case, all chicken grow on wood. I have sometimes spotted one that looked like it was growing in a lawn, but closer inspection revealed that it was growing on a stump or buried log.

Chicken of the woods usually has many individual caps arranged in shelf-like layers, or in a rosette. These caps are up to 3 cm thick with yellow pores rather than gills on their undersides. The orange, yellow, or white with yellow or orange upper surfaces are velvety. When you break a piece open, the flesh is white to pale yellow.

Bright orange or yellow and often growing halfway up a tree, "chicken" is one of the easiest to identify mushrooms and one of the tastiest.

HARVEST

Chicken of the woods is a parasite mushroom that can eventually kill its host tree. You are not endangering the mushroom species or the tree by harvesting chicken. Harvest by slicing off the chicken just slightly away from the wood it is attached to. The best time to harvest this mushroom is when it is still young and moist rather than slightly dry and chalky, but you can find good culinary uses for older chickens as well.

PREPARE

A young chicken of the woods mushroom is fantastic simply sautéed in butter or oil with a little garlic and herbs of your choosing. You can also bake this mushroom or turn it into soup. Older mushrooms are best dried before using.

PRESERVE

Young chicken can be cooked and then frozen, pressure canned, or dehydrated. Older chicken of the woods never becomes tender when cooked, but it is still full of flavor. Dehydrate the mushrooms, grind in an electric grinder, and add the flavor-boosting powder to soups, gravies, and risotto.

RULE BREAKER

TURKEY TAIL MUSHROOM (*Trametes versicolor*)

I used to curse turkey tail mushrooms because they were by far the most abundant mushroom in my old stomping grounds of Brooklyn, New York. On good days I might find maitake, chicken of the woods, oyster, and many other choice mushrooms. But I could find turkey tail any day, and I had no use for it. Turkey tail mushrooms are too tough and leathery to be good to eat. Or so I thought.

Then I learned that a few fellow foragers were using this mushroom as a flavoring rather than a main ingredient. And that it is prized in other parts of the world for its medicinal benefits. I experimented with turkey tail—with tasty results—and decided to celebrate rather than curse its abundance. In addition to bringing excellent flavor to the party, turkey tail mushrooms are used medicinally to stimulate the immune system. They have also been used as an anti-cancer remedy.

Turkey tail mushrooms are common year-round, and while their texture is too tough to eat, their flavor and health benefits merit attention.

FIND AND IDENTIFY

Look for turkey tail mushrooms on fallen logs and stumps (these fungi are decomposers that break down cellulose and lignin in dead wood). They seem to be less moisture-dependent than other mushrooms, and it is often possible to find and harvest them even after a prolonged dry spell. Or maybe they have just dried out on the log when you find them—they will still be good for our purposes.

Turkey tail is a bracket mushroom, meaning it grows like little shelves. These shelves are thin, with a papery or leathery feel (unlike much larger, thicker hen of the woods, *Grifola frondosa*). Turkey tail's velvety surface can range from brown to brown-gray to reddish orange in concentric color zones that are, indeed, reminiscent of a turkey's tail.

Several other bracket fungi also meet this description so far. But here's how to tell that you've found the true turkey tail, *Trametes versicolor*. (And trust me: once you know how to identify this mushroom, you will see it frequently.) Look on the underside of the mushroom. Instead of a smooth pore surface like that of false turkey tail (*Stereum hirsutum*), or a sea sponge textured, lavender-colored underside like *Trichaptum abietinum*, turkey tail's underside reveals little holes or pits that look almost like the surface of coral. These are tiny tubes containing the mushroom's spores. Turkey tail's spore print is white to light yellow.

HARVEST

Use a sharp knife to cut turkey tail mushrooms from the rotting wood they are growing on. Don't tug or you'll dislodge the base along with dirt and debris that will be a hassle to remove if they get into your collection container.

PREPARE

You could boil turkey tail mushrooms for days and still have something as tough as the proverbial shoe leather. And no amount of mincing is going to give this mushroom a good mouthfeel. But the flavor is quite fine, making this a prime candidate for the "bay leaf method." Add fresh or dried turkey tail mushrooms to broths, sauces, and stews, but—as you would with bay leaves—remove them before serving.

You can also infuse them with other wild flavorings as an interesting component of wild beers and sodas. Dried and finely ground, turkey tails are a good addition to savory wild seasoning blends. Try combining them with the ground leaves of Northern bayberry, *Myrica pensylvanica* syn., *Morella pensylvanica*, and sweet fern, *Comptonia peregrina*. These aromatic herbs are also too tough to chew but packed with flavor.

PRESERVE

Turkey tail mushrooms are already quite dry when you harvest them, so fully dehydrating them is quick and easy. Just spread them out in a single layer at room temperature for a couple of days. If your environment is extremely humid, finish them off with a few minutes in an oven on its lowest setting. Or you can put them into a dehydrator for a few hours. Once dehydrated, store turkey tails in airtight containers. They keep indefinitely.

TOOTH MUSHROOMS

Mushrooms in this category have neither gills nor ridges (like chanterelles) nor pores. Instead, they have the fungal version of stalactites or icicles (whoever dubbed them tooth mushrooms must have been thinking of fangs rather than human teeth). Because of this feature, they are extremely easy to identify, making them good edibles for novice mushroom hunters. But novice or expert, you have reason to celebrate your find because they are one of the tastiest wild mushrooms.

Note the stalactite-like "teeth," rather than gills or pores, on these hedgehog mushrooms.

Tooth mushrooms include lion's mane mushrooms, which are in the *Hericium* genus and appear as whitish clumps of dangling "teeth" on hardwood trees, as well as hedgehog mushrooms, *Hydnum repandum* and *H. umbilicatum*. These are cap and stem mushrooms rather than stemless clumps. But look under the cap of a hedgehog and you'll see the ID-clinching teeth rather than gills or pores. Both *Hericium* and *Hydnum* mushrooms are choice wild edibles. To **harvest** tooth mushrooms, use a knife to slice the entire mushroom off near the base.

My favorite way to **prepare** these mushrooms is simply sautéed in a little butter or oil, with a dash of salt and pepper. Of course, you could add garlic or other seasonings, but tooth mushrooms have a delicate, almost sweet taste that shouldn't be overwhelmed with other flavors. They are good in egg dishes such as omelets and soufflés.

The best way I've found to **preserve** tooth mushrooms is to pan fry them in a little butter or oil and then freeze them. The solid base beneath the teeth may be sliced and dehydrated.

LION'S MANE (*Hericium americanum*)

This is one of my favorite edible wild mushrooms. It has been compared to scallops and lobster in texture and flavor, although it has a delicate mushroomy taste along with the seafood flavor notes.

FIND AND IDENTIFY

I'm using *Hericium americanum* here as the "true" lion's mane, but it can be difficult to distinguish this species from other tooth mushrooms in the same genus. (One tip: *Hericium americanum* does not branch, whereas other species in the genus do.) Not to worry: all the *Hericium* species you could possibly confuse with *H. americanum* are equally edible and delicious.

Look for lion's mane and other *Hericium* species from late summer through late autumn, less commonly in spring. They grow on hardwood trees; either on decaying logs, dying trees, or wounds on living trees (lion's mane is saprophytic, meaning it gets its nourishment from dead or decaying organic matter). These tooth mushrooms are easy to spot from a distance. See that white clump with many dangling white "teeth" halfway up that hardwood tree? There's your lion's mane. It has a white spore print.

Many edible mushrooms are also used as medicinals, and lion's mane is no exception. It boosts the immune system and has a positive effect on memory and overall brain health. Research is under way that suggests it may be helpful for Alzheimer's.

HARVEST

When lion's mane and other *Hericium* species start to turn tan or brown, they can have an unpleasant bitter taste. Ideally, you'll find a clump that is pure white. In that case, celebrate! You've just found a delicious wild mushroom, and all of it, including the dense base as well as the teeth, will be good.

Very young lion's mane mushrooms will look like lumps with very short teeth or bumps. They may have a pinkish color on the surface at this stage. If you find one of these lion's mane cubs you can either come back in a day or two and hope that no other forager beats you to it, or go ahead and harvest it (they are excellent at this stage).

If, on the other hand, you have found one that is just a little past prime, it will have fully elongated teeth that have started to turn tan, yellow, or brown on the tips of the teeth and overall outer surface. But don't be sad. If you cut

Lion's mane and other tooth mushrooms are not only easy to identify but have a sweet taste and seafood-like texture unmatched by other fungi.

away the teeth and the solid base behind them is white, that base may still be tasty enough to be worth harvesting.

Use a knife to cut the lion's mane away from the tree. Don't get greedy and cut too close to the bark of the tree or log, or you'll end up with a lot of debris that will be a pain to clean up before you cook the mushroom.

PREPARE

As with other tooth mushrooms, keep the other ingredients simple to showcase the delicate, slightly sweet taste of lion's mane. The texture is special, too, so don't chop it too finely. Lion's mane chowder is excellent. And I once cooked the simplest and best campfire meal by stuffing baked potatoes with lion's mane sautéed in a little salted butter.

PRESERVE

As with other tooth mushrooms, the best way to preserve lion's mane is to first cook and then freeze it. However, the meaty part of the mushroom just behind the teeth can be sliced and dehydrated with good results.

HOW TO TAKE A SPORE PRINT

Slice off the stipe. Place the mushroom's cap, underside down, on paper. Cover the mushroom cap with a glass or small bowl and leave for a few hours or overnight. Remove the glass or bowl. Carefully lift away the mushroom cap. The pattern you see on the paper is the spore print. Its color is a major factor in confirming mushroom identification.

It's useful to take two spore prints from two halves of the same mushroom, one on dark paper and one on light (construction paper works). Dark spore prints will show up better on light paper; white to cream or lavender spore prints will show up better on dark paper.

GILLED MUSHROOMS

I left this category for last because although many safe and delicious mushrooms have gills (including your average supermarket mushroom), gilled mushrooms are also the most deadly mushrooms out there.

If I was in that "lost in the woods" scenario and I found a mushroom that I did not know in either of the two categories above (cap and stem with pores; mushrooms without caps or stems), I might nibble a bit and spit it out if it was bitter. But if it had a cap and stem and gills, I wouldn't even chance that taste test. Nonetheless, many excellent edible mushrooms including oyster, wine cap, and meadow mushroom are in this category.

The best **harvesting** method is to slice the mushroom off at the base of the stipe (stem), leaving the mycelium intact in the ground. Take a spore print if you are not 100 percent certain of your ID.

My early training said to slice the mushroom off with a knife near the base, leaving the rest of the mushroom (the mycelium) intact to rejuvenate. This was supposed to be true for non-gilled mushrooms such as morels as well. Several long-term studies have shown, however, that the number of future fruiting bodies ("mushrooms") is not significantly impacted if harvesting is done by yanking the mushroom (and some of its underground mycelium) up.

But I continue to follow the "always slice, never yank" advice with mushrooms for a different reason: it makes cleanup easier, greatly shortening the time between harvest and dinner. The yank method brings soil into your harvest container, and all mushrooms have nooks and crannies for that soil—whose gritty unpleasantness you do not want in your meal—to hide in. Don't do it.

As with other edible mushrooms, most edible gilled mushrooms are good **prepared** by simply sautéing them in a little oil or butter. Enjoy as is, or once cooked, add to any recipe mushrooms are welcome in.

The best way to **preserve** edible gilled mushrooms is to first cook them in a little oil or butter and then freeze them. They are also good dehydrated, either in the sun or in a dehydrator or low oven (between 95°F and 125°F). They can then be reconstituted by soaking them in boiling hot water for 15 to 20 minutes (you will still need to cook them after you've reconstituted them). Save the soaking liquid to use in soups and gravies.

MEADOW MUSHROOM (*Agaricus campestris*)

FIND AND IDENTIFY

As their common name implies, meadow mushrooms like sunny lawns, meadows, and fields. They show up after rainfall in such locations, in autumn through early summer in mild winter areas, but in California sometimes year-round. They can grow on the ground singly, in "fairy rings," or groups (but not true clusters).

Meadow mushroom's pink gills are enclosed in a thin white membrane when young. They become dark brown when the mushroom matures, and the membrane breaks off into a rapidly disappearing ring on the stipe. Another important distinguishing identification characteristic is that the flesh is white throughout and it does *not* turn yellow when bruised.

HARVEST

Use a pocket or thumb knife to slice the stipe (stem) off just above soil level.

PREPARE

Enjoy *Agaricus campestris* cooked in any way you would cook its supermarket cousin *A. bisporus* (the ubiquitous grocery store mushroom), but do remember that it should not be eaten raw.

PRESERVE

Meadow mushrooms are good preserved by several methods. Once sliced, they can be sautéed and then frozen. They are good dehydrated. You can also salt cure them in layers with enough salt to cover each layer completely (soak salt-cured mushrooms for several hours before cooking). Another interesting way to preserve them is to first simmer 1-inch chunks of raw meadow mushrooms in full-strength vinegar for 5 minutes, drain, then pack into jars with aromatic herbs and cover with extra-virgin olive oil. Store in the refrigerator and be sure to take them out at least an hour before serving to come to room temperature. The result is like Italian marinated antipasto mushrooms.

Closely related to the familiar supermarket button mushroom (*Agaricus bisporus*), the meadow mushroom is one of the mostly widely eaten cap and stem, gilled mushrooms.

OYSTER MUSHROOM (*Pleurotus* species)

I call oyster mushrooms rule breakers because unlike most other shelf or bracket mushrooms, they have gills rather than pores on the undersides of the caps. And they sometimes, sort of, have stems. Chefs everywhere love these delicious, mild mushrooms, and they are one of the easiest to learn how to identify.

Oyster mushrooms grow in "shelves," but unlike most other mushrooms with that growth habit, oysters have gills rather than pores.

FIND AND IDENTIFY

Oyster mushrooms are usually found on hardwoods but occasionally on conifers. They are especially common on elm. *Pleurotus ostreatus* is a parasitic mushroom that causes white rot on dead and dying trees. It is also one of the rare carnivorous mushrooms with mycelia that are capable of killing and digesting nematodes.

The common name "oyster" comes from the shape of the fruiting body of these mushrooms. The rounded asymmetrical shape and stacked shelf growth habit of oyster, the mushroom, looks quite reminiscent of oyster, the mollusk. But the mushrooms are completely soft. Not only do they lack shells, they are not at all leathery like some other shelf or bracket mushrooms.

The cap colors range from off-white to gray to brown, but you'll usually only find one color on a particular cluster of oyster mushrooms. And that cluster can be hefty, sometimes more than 20 pounds.

Oysters don't always have stems, but when they do they are off-center. When there is a stem, the gills run most of the way down it to the point of attachment.

HARVEST

Come in with a sharp pocket knife and slice each oyster off the tree or log. Don't cut too close to the bark, or your cleanup will be harder when you get your haul home. When you harvest in this way you are leaving the mycelium in the wood, and subsequent flushes will often occur in the same spot in a few weeks or months. Remember your spots and check them often.

PREPARE

I'm trying to think of a way I *don't* like oyster mushrooms and I'm coming up short. Oysters will excel anywhere a gentle but pronounced mushroom flavor is welcome, whether sautéed, in risotto, in soups and stews, in omelets, on toast points, or in sauces. The texture once cooked is just slightly softer and silkier than supermarket button mushrooms.

PRESERVE

The best way to preserve oysters is to first cook and then freeze them. Second best, but still good, is to dehydrate them.

14

SEAWEEDS

SEA VEGETABLES ARE BELOVED staple foods in some coastal cultures but have been relatively ignored by others until recently. Because of their health benefits (high in minerals and fiber, good protein content, low in calories) and their sheer abundance, they are becoming increasingly common as commercially sold salads and snacks.

While many seaweeds can be **harvested** year-round, they usually have the best flavor when the water is cold, fall through spring. As with wild edibles that grow on land, pollution is something you must consider when harvesting sea vegetables. If the water is not clean, do not gather there. One way to know how clean (or not) the sea is where you want to forage is to check in with local commercial fishermen who usually have the water tested on a regular basis.

It is always a good idea to carry a sharp knife or scissors if you are planning to harvest seaweed. Rather than yanking the holdfast at the base off the seaweed off along with the rest of the algae, snip off the fronds leaving the holdfast behind. This will enable the seaweed to regenerate.

To **prepare** any kind of seaweed, first rinse it well to remove any sand and grit. Use fresh or rehydrated seaweed in salads (look to Japanese cuisine for

Harvest seaweed from shorelines with clean water.

WARNING While no seaweeds are poisonous, those that were growing at deeper than low tide lines are more likely to have absorbed toxins. These will only appear within your reach on the shore if they have detached from the ocean floor and washed up. For that reason, many foragers prefer to only harvest seaweed that is still attached to rock, seabed, or other seaweed.

dressings that go well with seaweed salads). Seaweeds are also good in soups, especially seafood-based soups.

You can use wide seaweed fronds to wrap other foods, rolling them up the way you would stuffed cabbage or dolmades but with a taste of the sea (try including some cooked fish and rice in the stuffing for a lovely combination). Or you can purée fresh or reconstituted seaweeds and then dehydrate the resulting mush as you would a thin fruit leather to make your own nori substitute for sushi.

When you harvest seaweed, leave the holdfast attached.

Especially wide seaweeds can be used instead of lasagna noodles; just keep in mind that they will have a strong impact on the flavor of the finished dish.

The best way to **preserve** seaweed is to dehydrate it. You can use a dehydrator, an oven on its lowest setting (prop the door open with a wooden spoon if the lowest setting is 150°F or more), or by hanging a clothesline in a dry space with good air circulation and attaching your seaweed harvest to it laundry-style. Once dehydrated, seaweed will keep indefinitely in tightly sealed jars, although it will lose some vitamin B content with time. To use, pour boiling hot water over the dried seaweed and let it soak until plump from rehydration. Drain and use.

Dried seaweed can also be toasted to make crunchy snacks (just as good as the seaweed snacks you can buy nowadays, and without all the plastic packaging).

DULSE (*Palmaria palmata*)

FIND AND IDENTIFY

You'll find dulse on rocky coastlines around the world, usually attached to rocks but occasionally attached to other seaweed species. Its scientific binomial, *Palmaria palmata*, gives a big clue to one of this seaweed's identification characteristics: like the palms of your hands, dulse fronds are one piece at the base. They divide into finger-like segments from that unified base (there is no consistency to the number of segments, though).

Dulse's hand-like fronds are flat and have a disc-shaped base called a holdfast. Sometimes extra "fingers" or "leaflets" emerge from the otherwise smooth margins. This is most common near the base. Most seaweeds are green, brown, or yellow, but dulse is a rich maroon color, which is one of its easiest-to-spot ID characteristics.

HARVEST

When it's low tide, dulse and other seaweeds will be exposed and easy to spot. Harvest only from a site with clean waters (verify by checking with approved fishing locations that have their waters frequently tested for pollution). Harvest dulse by slicing or snipping off the fronds with a knife or scissors. Do not just yank them up. Take some of the "palm" to hold the "fingers" together, but leave the lower 2 inches or so still attached to the rock or other seaweed.

PREPARE

I am not a huge fan of freshly harvested dulse eaten raw. But some foragers love it that way, so give it a try and find out if it agrees with your palate.

Commercially sold dulse goes through an enzymatic process that keeps it soft even when dried. I haven't yet been able to duplicate this at home, but it doesn't really matter because dried dulse is good crunchy or softened with a touch of water.

For crunchy dulse chips, heat a skillet over medium-high heat for 1 or 2 minutes, then add pieces of dulse (I use scissors to snip the dried dulse into chip-sized pieces). Cook for just a minute, stirring or tossing the entire time. Remove from the heat and let cool. You know how cookies develop their crunch after they come out of the oven and as they cool off? Same deal with your dulse

Dulse is an easy to identify seaweed found on several continents. Its flavor is less briny than that of many other seaweeds, making it a good entry bite into the world of sea vegetables for those who are skeptical.

NUTRITIONAL BENEFITS

You'll be adding a dose of B vitamins, especially B6, to any dish in which you include dulse. It will also boost your health with its fiber, protein, iodine, and potassium.

chips. But don't leave them out for more than an hour or they'll start to absorb the air's humidity and get soft again.

Dulse is superb added to seafood chowders and stews (or vegan sea-scented soups), combined with other seaweeds in salads, and anywhere a briny but slightly sweet flavor and gently chewy texture would be welcome. If the chewiness is an issue, finely chop the dulse and you won't notice it.

PRESERVE

In my opinion, the flavor of dulse really comes out when it is dried, even if it is then rehydrated. To dry dulse, rinse it off then spread it out in a single layer between two screens and put it out in the sun. If it is very humid in your neck of the woods, use a dehydrator instead (set it to 110°F). Whether sun-drying or using a dehydrator, dry the dulse until it is brittle (how long this will take will depend on the thickness of your dulse fronds).

As with other dehydrated foods, store dulse in airtight containers so that it doesn't absorb atmospheric moisture and invite mold. Correctly stored, dried dulse will keep forever, but its vitamin B content will decline with time.

PART THREE

Getting the Most Out of Your Wild Edibles

15

TROUBLESHOOTING FLAVOR FUMBLES

IT'S NOT UNCOMMON FOR WILD FOODS to have much stronger flavors than what you might be used to. This is partially because mainstream crops have often been bred specifically for bulk and blandness (think mild farm lettuces such as romaine versus the robust taste of wild lettuce or dock leaves).

With some wild edibles, timing is *the* factor that influences whether a wild edible will be tender and mild or tough and bitter. Dandelion greens in April can be fantastic, but I bet your face will pucker if you try them in August. A chicken of the woods mushroom at its recently emerged tender and juicy stage is a different animal—I mean, fungi—than the chalky, past-its-prime specimen just a few days later.

What is a forager to do when she finds a good wild edible to harvest, but it is slightly out of season or past its prime? Although my first advice is to pick whatever is at its seasonal peak on the day that you venture forth, there are some fixes for when wild ingredients are a bit too bitter, tough, fuzzy, flavorless, or astringent.

BUT IT'S SO BITTER

For most of the twentieth century, bland food was considered desirable, but in the twenty-first century, bitterness has been regaining favor, even in North America.

When your taste buds detect bitterness, they are detecting the presence of alkaloids, which are characteristically bitter. Many common wild foods including dandelion, dock, and chicory have a sliding scale of bitterness that relates to the weather. In cool weather, they are usually milder; on a hot summer day they may be so bitter that even someone with a very adventurous palate would spit them out.

Non-aromatic plants such as these often have medicinal properties that come from their alkaloid content (with aromatic plants, it's usually the intensely fragrant essential oils that carry the medicinal benefits). This means that when dock greens, for example, are at their least bitter in the cool weather of early spring and late fall, they are good food. But if you're harvesting their roots for medicinal value, you'd do better to gather them during the dog days of late summer and early fall when the bitterness of the entire plant—and therefore alkaloid content—is highest.

But let's say you've found a non-aromatic, bitter type of wild food that is right on the verge of being too bitter. Is it salvageable? Probably. Here are a few ways to deal with excess bitterness in wild leaves, stalks, and roots:

1. Boil and boil again. This is an old-fashioned way to deal with bitter wild vegetables. Boil them, drain them, boil them in a fresh pot of water, drain again, and repeat until the bitterness is reduced to something you can tolerate. Unfortunately, this method also destroys much of the nutritional value of the food and reduces its texture to mush. I am not a fan, so I recommend the following two methods.

2. Augment with other strong flavors. This is akin to meeting fire with fire. Got bitterness? Match it with vinegar or lemon juice (sourness), toss with bacon (saltiness, umami), even add a drizzle of honey or syrup (sweetness) to the mix. These are classic ways to offset bitterness. In fact, bitterness becomes just another player at the party

rather than something you are trying to avoid. It's effective, but if you're primary ingredient was really, *really* on the south side of bitter, I recommend the next method.

3. Boil, then augment. Get some water boiling. Add your bitter wild food and boil for less than 5 minutes (3 is my usual). Drain. Put the parboiled ingredient in a skillet with a splash of balsamic, a bit of bacon, or another augmenting flavor. Cook for a few more minutes and enjoy.

TOO TOUGH TO CHEW

This one is easy to get around. Here are four methods I recommend:

1. Very finely chop, then combine with less toothsome ingredients. Fibrous roots can mostly be avoided by learning at what stage and time of year to harvest them, but if you have them, mince and add to muffins and quick breads or even stews. Minced leaves disappear into soups and stews, adding nutrition rather than texture.

2. Bake or dehydrate tough leaves into chips. They will be pleasantly crunchy rather than chewy.

Larger first-year garlic mustard leaves can be a bit bitter and veiny, but dehydrating them into chips turns them into a culinary treat.

3. Massaged salads are another great way to work around tough leaf and root textures. Thinly slice the ingredients (leaves into ribbons, roots into paper-thin slivers). Drizzle with vinegar or lemon or lime juice, and massage. Yes, literally squeeze and rub the vegetables until they wilt, almost as if they were cooked. Sprinkle with salt, add other salad ingredients as desired, and serve.

4. Follow what I call the "bay leaf method." If a leaf, mushroom, or other wild edible is too tough to chew but has terrific flavor, add it to the soup or sauce pot but remove it before serving.

These older field garlic leaves are tough but still have good garlicky flavor. Tying them in a knot makes it easier to remove them from the pot before serving.

FUZZY IS NOT A CHOICE CULINARY TEXTURE

Many leaves have a coarse or fuzzy texture that is not good eats. You could use the same work-arounds as for tough to chew food, but that is only necessary when making a raw salad. Once cooked, the fuzziness of leaves disappears.

NO FLAVOR

As someone who has cooked with wild foods for most of my life, I can testify that "bland" wild foods can be an asset. First, remember that texture is its own culinary category. Those cattail rhizomes may not knock out your taste buds with intense flavor, but their excellent texture is a perfect foil for that elderberry-balsamic drizzle sauce. Mild wild foods can also tone down others that are a bit too strongly flavored. For example, add some clearweed (*Pilea pumila*) to that slightly-too-bitter shredded broad-leaved dock (*Rumex obtusifolius*) in your salad.

TOO ASTRINGENT

When you bite into an unripe crabapple and your mouth goes instantly dry and your entire face puckers in reaction, that is astringency. It is a totally different experience from sourness, which can make you salivate rather than the opposite.

Astringency is almost always a case of harvesting too soon. In addition to crabapples, numerous other wild fruits including silverberry (*Elaeagnus*) and American persimmon (*Diospyros virginiana*) are unpleasantly astringent if you bite into them before they are ripe.

Note that unleached acorns have a similarly awful, puckery mouthfeel, but with them the high tannin content is responsible. No amount of waiting for the acorns to ripen (any more than they already have when they fall off the tree) will help. Leaching out the tannins is the only answer.

TRANSLATING OLDER
WILD FOOD FIELD GUIDES

I have already urged you to use this book as a cross-reference with reliable field guides. If, however, the field guides you've got were written before the turn of the millennium, you will run into a few potentially confusing patterns.

One of these is the habit of describing the plant as it will be at maturity rather than during its differing stages of growth. So, for example, you might read about mugwort: "Pointy, sharply divided leaves on 4- to 6-foot stalks." Except that in early spring mugwort plants are only a few inches high and the divided leaves are more rounded than pointy. Remember that all plants start out small, and that leaf shape can vary even on the same plant.

Don't even get me started with cooking metaphors! Chicory leaves are not at all "like spinach," Japanese knotweed shoots are not "like asparagus," and daylily buds are not "like green beans." And yet you will see such analogies repeated again and again in foraging literature. These are not totally wrong, just misleading. What they are referring to is the part of the plant and, sometimes, appropriate cooking methods. For example, although chicory leaves have a bitter edge nothing like spinach, similar cooking methods and times apply. Lightly oniony daylily buds are approximately the same thickness as green beans and may be cooked similarly. Japanese knotweed, like asparagus, emerges in spring as an edible shoot that regrows each year from perennial roots. What is confusing is that if you tell someone to cook chicory leaves "like spinach," they are likely to think it is going to taste "like spinach," which it most certainly will not.

Flavors and fragrances are notoriously difficult to describe—imagine that you are trying to describe cinnamon to someone who had never smelled or tasted cinnamon. How would you even begin? So take all wild food flavor descriptions (including mine) with a grain of salt. What does a burdock root taste like? A burdock root.

16

UNIVERSAL
WILD FOOD RECIPES

IF YOU HAVE A STARTER TECHNIQUE with any wild food, you can then embellish to your heart's delight, creating infinite variations on that already delicious foundation. Or just leave it alone. Did I mention that simple is good?

I hesitated to include the word "recipes" in this chapter's title, because these are really just simple techniques every forager should know. (Of course, they work just as well with tame foods.) But one of the delightful challenges of working with wild foods is that you, the cook, are on the road less traveled. You will need to improvise, trust your taste buds, find out what works for you. These basic recipes will make it easier for you to do that.

LEAFY GREENS FOUR WAYS

Salads (No, It's Not as Simple as That)

In theory, a salad of wild leafy greens should be as simple as washing some leaves and tossing them with a little dressing. With never-bitter, smooth-textured leaves such as those of Asiatic dayflower or purslane this is true.

But what about fuzzy leaves like mallow, stringy ones like plantain, or ones like dock that you harvested at their seasonal verge of too bitter to be good?

Wild raw leaves and veggies sometimes need slightly different treatment than their culti-vated counterparts.

Fuzzy, stringy, and extremely bitter are not desirable in a salad. You can con-quer fuzziness and stringiness by cooking, and once cooked, the greens can be served as a salad at room temperature with any dressing you like. If you are determined to serve fuzzy and stringy leaves raw, finely chop or slice them into very thin ribbons before combining with other salad ingredients.

If bitterness is the issue, combine the finely chopped leaves with milder ingredients, or boil them first and squeeze out as much moisture as possible before crumbling the wad of cooked greens into your salad. (This description will make sense as soon as you try it for the first time.)

And one more trick with creds to John Kallas, who mentions it in his book *Edible Wild Plants*. Some wild greens (lamb's quarters, violet leaves, garlic mustard leaves) stick together once tossed with salad dressing. This creates a dense and somewhat unappealing mass. But if you leave a little bit—maybe a ¼ inch—of stem on each leaf, the salad remains fluffy rather than compacted.

A Mess o' Greens (Cooked Wild Leafy Greens)

Here is one of the simplest ways to cook wild greens. This won't help with extreme bitterness or astringency, but it does eliminate any fuzziness or coarse textures (amaranth, mallow, etc.). If the texture issue with your wild leafy greens is stringiness rather than fuzziness, simply chop them finely before cooking them.

Wild greens
Optional seasonings such as salt, pepper, garlic, butter, or olive oil

---

Pick through your wild edible leaves, removing any discolored ones or tough stems. Wash them well, then toss them into a hot pot or pan with just the water clinging to them. Stir over medium-high heat until wilted. If the pan starts to dry out before the greens are fully wilted, add a scant tablespoon of water. Remove from heat, add seasonings of your choosing, and serve hot or at room temperature.

If the leaves are a tad too bitter for your taste, first bring a pot of water to a boil. Add the leaves and boil for 3 minutes. Drain. Sauté the blanched leaves in a little oil or butter with garlic or another seasoning for an additional 3 to 5 minutes.

Matching Strong Flavors for Balanced Flavor

The classic way to tame the tastes of some wild greens is to add other strong flavors into the mix until you end up with an appealing balance. A classic French way to prepare dandelion greens is to cook them with some bacon and a splash of vinegar. The saltiness and umami of the bacon join with the sourness of the vinegar and meet the bitterness of the dandelion as equals, rendering it an appealing rather than off-putting taste. A spoonful of sweetness is another way to complement intense wild tastes and will go a long way toward balancing bitterness.

Combine and experiment with my go-to ingredients for meeting strong flavors in wild greens.

Wild greens

**Soy sauce or tamari; garlic; lemon juice, vinegar, or verjus; sweeteners
(sugar, honey, agave, or maple syrup); hot sauce or hot chili peppers**

Bacon (optional)

Cook the greens until they are wilted in a little water, butter, or oil. Then add a
dash of any of the condiments mentioned—or a combination of them—to taste.

Leaf Chips

This method tames both stringiness and bitterness.

Large wild leaves such as those of plantain, garlic mustard, and broad-leaved dock

Extra-virgin olive oil or other oil

Salt

**Powdered seasonings such as wild garlic, cayenne, peppergrass,
nutritional yeast, ground cumin, or ground garlic mustard seeds**

Wash your wild edible leaves and dry them in
a salad spinner or by rolling them up in a dish
towel. Toss them with a little bit of oil and a
sprinkle of salt and other powdered seasonings
of your choice.

If using an oven, spread the leaves on baking
sheets in a single layer (it's okay if the leaves
overlap slightly, but they shouldn't be piled on
top of one another). Bake at 200°F until crispy
but not burnt. This can take as little as 8 minutes. If using a dehydrator, arrange the leaves
on the dehydrator trays so that they barely overlap. Dehydrate at anywhere
between 115°F and 135°F until crispy, which takes longer in a dehydrator
than an oven (as long as several hours).

Universal Five Diamonds Salad Recipe

This salad is a meal unto itself—you need nothing else except maybe some good bread. The recipe is named in part for the restaurant in Paris—Cinq Diamants—where I first learned the method, and for the five tastes (salty, sour, sweet, bitter, umami) that it includes. It also has a wonderful mix of soft, crunchy, and chewy textures.

I've given the amounts here as parts rather than measured quantities. Who knows how many salad greens you foraged today or how many people will show up at your table? But even these ratios are approximate. Experiment and find out what you love best. The important thing is to make sure all of the tastes and textures are represented in your salad bowl.

---

4 parts mild-flavored leaves

2 parts slightly bitter or more strongly flavored leaves

1 part onions, ramps, or any wild edible *Allium*

1 part something salty and umami (cheese, bacon, sautéed mushrooms)

1 part dried fruit

1 part something crunchy (nuts, seeds)

Extra-virgin olive oil

Lemon juice, vinegar, or pickle juice

Salt and pepper

Wash the leaves and dry them in a salad spinner or by rolling them up in a clean dish towel(s). Peel and thinly slice the onion or other *Allium*. Place in a large bowl along with the salty, fruity, and crunchy ingredients. Drizzle over the olive oil and lemon juice to taste, season with salt and pepper to taste, and toss to combine. You can also plate individually by tossing the greens with the oil and sour component, distributing the dressed leaves between plates or bowls, and then topping with the other ingredients.

MORE UNIVERSAL RECIPES:
MUSHROOMS, ROOTS, SOUP, AND FLOUR

Simply Sautéed Wild Mushrooms

The beauty of this method is that the final product is so versatile. Once cooked, mushrooms prepared this way freeze perfectly. Or eat them as is, serve on a cracker, or purée into a spread. They also make a great addition to pasta, pizza, risotto, and so much more.

Butter or oil
Wild mushrooms, chopped or sliced
Garlic, salt, pepper, or seasonings of choice

Heat the butter or oil in a pan over medium-low heat. Be generous with the lipid: there should be enough butter or oil to completely coat the bottom of the pan. Add the mushrooms and cook, stirring often, until the mushrooms release their liquid. Continue to cook, stirring, until the liquid is mostly reabsorbed or evaporated. Add garlic, salt, pepper, or any other seasoning of your choice.

Universal Taproots and Tubers Recipe

This utterly delicious recipe is simple enough to do in a pot or skillet over a campfire. The vegetables come out tender and coated with a lightly sweet glaze. It is a fantastic way to prepare Jerusalem artichoke or daylily tubers, as well as burdock taproots. This is not a good recipe to use with very fibrous roots as the cooking time is relatively short.

Feel free to adjust the quantities listed to reflect the amount of roots and tubers you're cooking.

1½ pounds edible taproots and/or tubers
1 tablespoon butter, coconut oil, or other lipid
2 teaspoons sugar, honey, maple sugar, or other sweetener
Salt and pepper
Note: Ground spicebush or melilot are good additions if you've got them. Of the more conventional spices, a tiny bit of freshly ground nutmeg is excellent here.

Peel the roots or tubers if necessary (otherwise, just scrub clean). Chop into pieces no thicker than ½ inch.

Put the chopped vegetables into a pot or skillet along with the butter and sugar. Add enough water to just cover. Simmer until the vegetables are fork tender (easily pierced with a fork) and the water has evaporated completely. How long this will take depends on what species of root vegetable you are cooking. If the food is not yet tender and the water is already about to be gone, add a little more water.

Season with salt and pepper to taste, and serve immediately.

Wild Vegetable Soup

This adaptable recipe can be made with almost any wild edible vegetables. It is good chunky or puréed. If puréed, serve it hot or cold. Choice your seasonings and toppings depending on what tastes good to you with the wild vegetables you began with.

---

3 parts wild root vegetables or shoots or edible flower stalks

1 part any *Allium* leaves or bulbs, minced

1 part wild or cultivated edible Apiaceae leaves, such as goutweed, wild fennel, celery, parsley (emphasis on edible—remember that this plant family contains extremely poisonous plants), finely chopped

Water, vegetable stock, or animal stock

4 parts mildly flavored wild greens cleaned and coarsely chopped

Salt, ground black pepper, peppergrass seeds, and/or garlic mustard seeds

Edible flowers for garnish

Combine the root vegetables, *Allium* leaves or bulbs, and Apiaceae leaves in a pot over high heat. Add water or stock to slightly more than cover the other ingredients. Cover the pot and bring the soup to a boil. Remove cover, reduce heat, and simmer until the root vegetables are almost tender. How long that will take depends on the species of root vegetable you are cooking and how tender of a stage they were at when you harvested them. Add more liquid if necessary. Add the greens and seasonings to taste, and cook until everything is very soft. Serve as is, or purée first.

Wild asparagus and redbud blossoms make this soup something only a forager can experience.

Garnish with any of the wild ingredients, such as a few steamed wild aspara-gus spears, or wild edible flowers in season (such as the redbud blossoms).

Making Flour from Wild Foods

The obvious candidates for making flour are grains such as wild rice, or seeds such as amaranth, dock, and plantain. You can also make flour from dried wild edible tubers or from nuts. Actually, any dehydrated food including leaves such as nettles and even powdered mushrooms can be used as a "flour."

If you're making bread, remember that none of these wild ingredients has the gluten of wheat. This means that if you use 100 percent alternative flour—flour made from ingredients other than wheat—it will not rise the same way that wheat dough does. But you can replace at least 25 percent of the wheat flour with a wild flour and still end up with a lovely bread. And in recipes where a rise is not necessary, such as crackers, you can go with 100 percent wild flour.

To make flour out of wild seeds, leaves, grains, or roots, first dry them completely in a dehydrator or oven. Let cool, then grind in an electric coffee grinder. Store in tightly sealed glass jars for up to 3 months. For longer storage, keep them in airtight containers in the refrigerator or freezer.

Flowers as flour: here red clover flowers are used to replace some of the wheat flour in a soda bread recipe.

17

PRESERVING WILD FOODS

EVERY FORAGER I KNOW IS, or eventually becomes, interested in food preservation to some degree. This is not a coincidence. In traditional cultures, and even in nomadic cultures, food preservation has always been part of the mix that makes up a sustainable food system. This is not just a matter of stockpiling food to get through the winter in cold winter regions. It is also about well-rounded nutrition and keeping meals interesting.

But never mind traditional cultures: let's look at how foraging and food preservation fit together in the twenty-first century. Let's say it is January and I'm in New York. There is a scant number of fresh wild edibles peeping out from the snow. You could go for bark or pine needles, but basically it is not peak foraging season. Do you, as a forager, starve?

No, of course not. Nor is your food going to be boring. You've got wild blueberries from last July in your freezer to go into your breakfast smoothie, along with hazelnut milk from nuts harvested in September. When summer comes again, you can make griddle cakes with your frozen acorn flour to go with fresh wineberries. The combination of freshly picked foraged ingredients with preserved ones makes your meal much more well-rounded and delectable.

Many wild edibles have extremely short seasons, even more so than cultivated crops. Preserving some of your wild harvest enables you to enjoy black raspberries, for example, year-round rather than for just a couple of weeks in June.

HOW FOOD PRESERVATION WORKS

Every method of food preservation is based on the fact that bacteria and molds that could be dangerous to eat are prima donnas. In other words, they can only survive in a very narrow range of conditions. They cannot survive environments that are too hot, too cold, too dry, too acidic, or too alkaline. When we preserve wild foods (or any foods) we are tweaking one or more of these factors to eliminate harmful bacteria and mold.

This section provides just the basics of what I consider to be some of the most useful forms of food preservation for wild edibles. Check out the resources section to find more in-depth information on preserving food safely.

Dehydrating

Dried wild apples are a tasty snack and also useful in compotes, granola, and trail snack mixes.

Drying is probably the oldest form of food preservation. It works well with most wild foods from mushrooms to leaves, berries, roots, barks, and aromatic flowers such as bee balm (*Monarda*) and basswood (*Tilia*). One wild edible that is *not* a good candidate for dehydrating is purslane (*Portulaca oleracea*). Purslane's succulent stems and leaves are better suited for pickling.

Slice or chop the food into pieces no thicker than ½ inch. Arrange them on dehydrator baking trays in a single layer, without too much overlapping.

For fruits and vegetables that brown when exposed to air (such as wild apples, pears, and burdock "cardoons"), dip them in acidified water before dehydrating. Just add a couple of tablespoons of vinegar or lemon juice to a gallon of water, and drop the food into the liquid as you chop it up. Green vegetables will keep their color best if first blanched in boiling water for a minute then quickly chilled in cold water before dehydrating.

You will get the best results with a dehydrator, but it is not essential to use one. An oven on its lowest setting works (if that is hotter than 150°F, prop the oven door open with a wooden spoon). Just expect that oven-dehydrated foods tend to darken and lose more color than those dried in a dehydrator.

If you live in an arid region, you may be able to sun-dry foods. Simply place them in between screens to keep out insects, and bring them indoors at night because even desert areas may have morning dew.

Lacto-Fermentation

Lacto-fermentation is the process that creates sauerkraut, real deli dill pickles, and kimchi. After dehydrating, it is one of the oldest known forms of food preservation. All you need is salt, raw food, and sometimes water. (Note that lacto-fermentation is sometimes called "pickling," but the process is very different from making vinegar pickles.)

The way it works is that there are good-for-us probiotic bacteria that are salt tolerant. The dangerous bacteria are not. So you start out by immersing the food in a salt brine that is strong enough to kill off the bad guys but mild enough that the good guy probiotics aren't bothered. Those good guy bacteria then go to work on the food, eventually creating a deliciously sour environment that is too acidic for any dangerous bacteria to move in. There's much more to learn about fermentation, of course, and I urge you to check out the recommended books in the resources section.

Here's a simple way to ferment any wild food that can be eaten raw.

WARNING Do not ferment foods that need to be cooked to be safe, such as pokeweed (*Phytolacca americana*) and wild mushrooms. Cooked food won't ferment because the heat of cooking kills off the good guy bacteria along with the bad guys.

Universal Probiotic Fermented Pickle Recipe

These pickles are not only healthy, they are also delicious. This is a great opportunity for culinary experimentation. You can mince your ingredients for a probiotic relish, leave them chunky for a sturdier pickle, or get creative with the seasonings. Those are just a few ideas to get you started.

Purslane's succulent, naturally tart stems make fabulous fermented pickles.

Note that if the temperature is above 75°F, fermentation can get sluggish and mold may move in. I add a pinch of extra salt during summer's hottest months.

---

2 cups chopped wild vegetables
2 teaspoons sea, kosher, or other non-iodized salt
1 clove garlic or 1 teaspoon chopped edible *Allium* of your choice
1 teaspoon peppergrass, spicebush, mustard seeds, or other spice

---

Toss the wild vegetables with the salt and seasonings and pack into clean glass jars or ceramic crocks. Let sit for 30 minutes. If enough liquid has been drawn out of the food to cover the solids, you're ready for the next step. If not, add some filtered or non-chlorinated water. (Avoid chlorinated tap water, which could kill off the healthy bacteria that you need for a successful fermentation.)

Place a large edible leaf such as a wild grape leaf or a dock leaf on top of the other ingredients, and tuck the edges down between the food and the sides of the jar. You're using the leaf to keep the food completely submerged in the brine. Alternatively, place a well-washed stone on top of the food for the same purpose.

Cover with a loose lid or a clean cloth. Place the jar on a plate to catch the overflow that usually occurs during the first days of fermentation. Leave it out at room temperature for 3 to 14 days. Check your ferment daily. You should start to see frothy bubbles on top, especially when you press down on the ingredients. A clean, pleasantly sour smell should develop. Taste your ferment. When it is sour enough for you, transfer it to the refrigerator to slow down the fermentation. The ferment will keep indefinitely in the refrigerator but will become more sour in flavor and softer in texture the longer you keep it.

Vinegar Pickling

Vinegar pickling preserves any food because it is based on a brine with such a low pH that harmful bacteria cannot survive. You can dilute any vinegar with an acetic acid content of 4.5 percent or higher with an equal amount of water and end up with a brine for pickles that you can store in sealed jars at room temperature. If you dilute the vinegar more than that, you need to store the pickles in the refrigerator. If you are using homemade vinegar, you will need to test it to find out its percentage of acetic acid.

Some of my favorite wild pickle ingredients are wild asparagus, immature milkweed florets, fat purslane stems, beach plums, wild carrot young flower stalks (peeled), green black walnuts, and daylily buds.

My favorite vinegar pickle recipe is for a refrigerator pickle. I prefer the lighter vinegar taste because it doesn't drown out the flavors of the wild foods.

My Favorite Pickle Anything Recipe

My family loves these pickles so much that I make a jar or two every week. The amount of vinegar is fairly low, which creates a light flavor and leaves the wild foods with good textures. However, because of the low amount of vinegar, these pickles are not suitable for canning and must be stored in the refrigerator.

---

2 cups any wild vegetable or fruit that is safe to eat raw

1 tablespoon of any wild or cultivated garlic, bulbs left whole

2 teaspoons pickling spice (peppergrass or wild mustard seeds are great)

2 sprigs fresh wild fennel fronds or dill or another leafy aromatic herb

2 cups water

¼ cup plus 2 tablespoons apple cider vinegar

1 tablespoon sea, kosher, or other non-iodized salt

1½ tablespoons sugar, or 1 tablespoon honey

Pack the vegetable or fruit into a clean glass jar, tucking in the garlic, spices, and herbs as you go.

Bring the water, vinegar, salt, and sugar to a boil. Stir to dissolve the salt and sugar.

Pour the hot brine over the other ingredients, making sure they are completely covered. You will probably have some leftover pickling liquid, but on the off chance that there isn't enough to cover the solid food, mix up some more using the same ratio of water, vinegar, salt, and sugar (you can save any leftover pickling liquid for future pickles). Secure the lid. Let the jar cool until barely warm before transferring to the refrigerator. Wait at least 3 days for the flavors to develop before enjoying your wild pickles.

For a version that may be processed in a boiling water bath for storage at room temperature, increase the amount of vinegar to 1 cup and decrease the amount of water to 1 cup. This will result in a sharper-tasting pickle, so you may want to add a little extra sugar to buffer the sourness. Do not reduce the amount of vinegar, as that is your safety provider in this recipe.

Freezing and Blanching

Freezing is a fantastic way to preserve nuts, fruits, mushrooms (best if cooked before they are frozen, though there are some exceptions), and most vegetables if they are blanched first.

The downsides of freezing wild food are (1) you need electricity, and (2) you need space (many foragers and hunters have two or even three freezers). Two kinds of wild food that I do *not* recommend freezing are root vegetables, with the exception of bulbs, and thin-leaved aromatic herbs.

Blanching before freezing just means briefly exposing an ingredient to boiling water. What this does is halt the enzymatic processes that continue in the freezer with raw ingredients (freezing temperatures kill off and prevent bacteria, mold, and grubs, but they do not destroy enzymes). If you've ever put a bunch of raw basil into the freezer and then tried to use it later, you know what I mean: it thawed to a dark, slimy mess. Blanching would have prevented that.

To blanch, first bring a pot of water to a boil. Add prepped (cleaned, peeled if necessary, chopped) wild food to the pot for 1 to 2 minutes. Drain and then immediately put the steaming blanched wild food into ice water or run it under very cold water. The cold water keeps it from continuing to cook from the residual heat (remember: you're not trying to cook the vegetables, just kill off those enzymes). Squeeze out as much water as possible before putting your blanched wild vegetables into freezer bags or containers, labeling, and freezing.

Note that wild fruits do not need to be blanched before they are frozen. However, see the individual types in chapter 9 for more detailed instructions.

Canning

When I teach workshops on preserving wild foods an astonishing number of people show up assuming it is going to be a canning workshop. Canning is one of the most recent methods of food preservation, and arguably my least favorite. Don't get me wrong: I still do a lot of canning of foods both wild and tame, but some pros and cons should be considered.

Pros: If you want to be able to store un-pickled, moist foods at room temperature, canning is the best option. Canned foods can be stored indefinitely (and there's no problem if the electricity goes out). It is also utterly convenient. I appreciate this when popping open an aromatic mix of wild mushroom, milkweed floret, and bee balm in a pasta sauce on a night that I don't feel like cooking, for example.

Cons: Canning results in greater loss of vitamins than most other food preservation methods. Secondly, plain canned wild vegetables are just as mushy and lackluster as store-bought, farm-grown ones. And as with frozen food, canned foods take up a lot of room and are heavy, making them impractical for backpacking trips (or very small kitchens and pantries).

Boiling Water Bath Canning vs. Pressure Canning

The most important thing to know about canning is that there are two distinctly different kinds: (1) boiling water bath canning and (2) pressure canning. Boiling water bath canning is low-tech but only suitable for a narrow range of foods. Pressure canning requires specialized gear but is essential for foods that do not qualify for boiling water bath canning. Here are the important distinctions:

Boiling water bath canning may be done with no more equipment than a big deep pot and some canning jars. But it is only safe with acidic foods, which include many fruits and all pickled foods with a low enough pH. So, for example, you may safely can blueberries or pickled wild asparagus in a boiling water bath, but for *un*-pickled wild asparagus you would need to use a pressure canner for a safe result. Non-acidic, un-pickled foods *must* be canned in a pressure canner, or there is a real risk of deadly botulism.

I realize this is not a detailed how-to guide for canning, as that's more than this book can encompass. You'll find many charts and detailed instructions online, as well as in my own and others' books (see the resources) that will tell you which foods work with which canning method. But most of them don't focus on wild foods. Here's a short breakdown of which wild foods are safe to preserve with a boiling water bath and which you really need to pressure can:

- Berries, tree fruits, and pickled vegetables with a pH of 4.6 or less are safe for boiling water bath canning (you can buy gear to test the pH of your wild foods at home, or look at some pickle brine recipes online that are specifically intended for canning to give you an idea of how that works).

- Un-pickled, non-acidic foods including all leaves, roots, shoots, stalks, flowers, and mushrooms must either be pickled for boiling water bath processing, or pressure canned. This also would apply to nuts and seaweed, except why would you want to can those great wild foods that are so perfect for drying or freezing?

Wild Soda, Wild Wine, Wild Vinegar

It is easy to make naturally sparkling sodas, wild wines, and (with a little patience) tangy wild vinegars. They all begin with exactly the same technique.

Give wild yeasts some sugar to work on, and they will start converting that sugar into ethanol (alcohol). At first, the alcohol will be minimal, the drink will be sweet, and the carbon dioxide produced by the process will give you a naturally fizzy soda. Let the yeasts keep doing their job on the sugar (sugar which could be from wild fruit juices or from granulated sugar you added—remember that the sugar is for the yeasts, not for you). After a while, the bubbliness will settle down while the alcohol content rises. Let the brew ferment out until still (no bubbles), and now you've got wild wine. Introduce acetic acid bacteria and let them have at the ethanol (alcohol) in your wine, and they will convert it into acetic acid. At 4 to 10 percent acetic acid, your brew now qualifies as vinegar (all vinegar begins as an alcoholic liquid).

So the process begins the same way whether your intended final product is a fizzy soda, a wine, or a gourmet vinegar. Here's how to get started:

Wild Soda and Wine (and Maybe Vinegar)

Start with a flavorful liquid. This could be juice from wild fruits such as apples, cherries, or grapes. Or skip the fruit and make an infusion of aromatic plants such as spruce (*Picea*), pineappleweed (*Matricaria matricarioides* syn. *M. discoidea*), or mugwort (*Artemisia vulgaris*). Even if you are using pure fruit juice, it is unlikely that there will be enough natural sugar in wild fruits (even grapes) for the kind of fermentation you're looking for, so you'll have to add some sugar. Remember that the sugar is not for you; it is for the wild yeasts. Here is the basic formula that I use:

---

1 gallon juice or water infused with aromatics
1 pound granulated sugar
3 tablespoons lemon juice or pasteurized vinegar
Wild yeast-bearing ingredients (see below)

Pour the juice or infusion into a clean bowl or crock. Add the sugar and stir to dissolve. Stir in the lemon juice or vinegar (pasteurized because you don't want to introduce live acetic acid bacteria just yet).

Add your wild yeast. My favorite sources of wild yeasts are a handful of unwashed fresh or frozen wild grapes (*Vitex*) or other fruit with a whitish "bloom" (that bloom *is* wild yeast), a few clusters' worth of elderberry flowers (*Sambucus*), black raspberry (*Rubus occidentalis*) or jewelweed stems—all these are usually rich in wild yeasts.

Cover your container with a clean cloth to keep out bugs. Leave at room temperature. Stir vigorously at least twice a day (more often is better). Within 1 to 3 days, you should start to see the mixture foam up when you stir it. This is a sign that fermentation is underway.

Strain the liquid. If you're going for a bubbly, slightly sweet beverage, transfer it immediately to sterilized plastic bottles. Cap tightly, refrigerate for 2 to 3 weeks, burping the bottles (opening the caps) occasionally so that they don't explode. Pour, sip, enjoy.

If you'd rather go for a drier, non-fizzy wine, pour the strained brew into a sterilized 1-gallon jug. Top the jug with a fermentation lock (see the resources) or a balloon that you've pricked once with a pin. The lock or balloon will allow gases to escape without letting contaminants in. When the balloon deflates, or the fermentation lock ceases to burble, you're ready to bottle. Siphon the wine into sterilized wine bottles, cork or cap, and age in a cool place. Some wild wines are ready to drink in just 3 months. Others (dandelion wine is a good example) transform from bearable to delicious if aged for at least 2 years.

Turn your wild wine into wild vinegar by pouring it back into a wide-mouthed vessel, such as a crock, and introducing a little raw vinegar. (If you're buying raw vinegar to kick-start your batch, look for one that says "with the mother" on the label. This means that it has active vinegar bacteria.) About a tablespoon of live, raw vinegar per pint of wine will be ample. Cover loosely with a cloth to keep out fruit flies. Stir vigorously several times a day for anywhere from 1 to 4 weeks until it has a strong sour smell and taste, then bottle and store in a cool place. Once you've got a batch of your own live vinegar going, you can use it as the starter culture for future batches of vinegar.

Infusing in Alcohol or Vinegar

Capture and preserve the flavor of any wild fruit or aromatic plant simply by soaking that wild ingredient in full-strength alcohol or vinegar for anywhere from 1 week to 1 month. Simply pack a clean glass jar with your featured ingredient, cover with the acidic or alcoholic liquid, and wait.

What does "full strength" mean? In the case of alcohol, I like to use neutrally flavored spirits that do not distract from the wild ingredients. Brandy or vodka (80 proof) works well. For vinegar, it should have an acetic acid content of 4.5 percent or higher. Almost all commercial vinegar does (and will say so on the label). If you are using homemade vinegar, you will need to test it to determine its acetic acid content.

A few of my favorite full-strength extractions are elderberry vinegar (tastes very similar to balsamic), mugwort vinegar (a mild-flavored but almost MSG-like—in a good way—flavor enhancer in marinades), pineappleweed cordial made with lightly sweetened infused vodka, and blackberry shrub made with sweetened blackberry vinegar added to cold sparkling water for a delicious summer drink.

Dry Salting

Burying food in layers of salt is a time-honored way of preserving foods but not common nowadays because so many people consider salt to be unhealthy. My own reason for not using this method is often less about health than space and resources—it takes a lot of salt to preserve a small amount of food this way, and the product is bulky while in storage. (One exception is verdurette, which is explained in the following recipe.)

The basic method is simple: Put a layer of salt in a container so that it completely covers the bottom of the container. Top that with a single layer of clean, dry, wild food (slice if the pieces are thicker than 1 inch). Cover the food completely with another layer of salt. Repeat for as many layers as you have food, and finish with a layer of salt.

Any wild vegetable or mushroom can be preserved this way indefinitely. To use your salt-preserved food, first soak it in several changes of water for at least an hour but as long as overnight, until it doesn't taste overly salty anymore.

Verdurette

Verdurette is the French name for a mix of salt with vegetables and herbs that can be used as the base for soups, dips, meat rubs, and more. It is a fantastic way to use odds and ends of wild foods—ones that you only found a little of, or that you harvested so much of that you won't be able to eat all the bounty fresh. I like to include a mix of aromatics (bee balm, honewort, etc.), alliums (field garlic, wild onion, etc.), wild root vegetables (wild carrot, burdock, etc.), and mild-flavored leafy greens (violet leaves, lamb's quarters, etc.).

Don't feel like you need to use up the last of your jar of wild verdurette before you start a new one. And if you don't have all the different categories of ingredients I mentioned, that is fine, too. I just make up a batch with whatever fresh ingredients I have, stir them up together with whatever was left in my verdurette jar, and put the jar back in the fridge. I also don't hesitate to combine wild with cultivated ingredients. So the taste of the verdurette changes with the seasonal ingredients I add, which I enjoy. As of this writing, my everlasting jar of wild verdurette has been seasoning my food for over two decades.

4 parts minced fresh wild vegetables and aromatic herbs (*see headnote*)
1 part sea, kosher, or other non-iodized medium-grain salt

Combine the wild vegetables, aromatic herbs, and salt. Pack into a clean glass jar, cover and store in the refrigerator or other cool place. Verdurette is ready to use immediately. When using verdurette, leave out any other salt in your recipe: you most likely won't need it.

ACKNOWLEDGMENTS

It has been my privilege during the past few decades to correspond with, sometimes meet in person, and learn from many skilled foragers including Stephan Barstow, Pascal Bauder, Wildman Steve Brill, Bill Cook, Greene Deane, Dan de Lion, Arthur Haines, Melana Hiatt, Michael Hood, Little John, John Kallas, Dawn Kirk, Gary Lincoff, Doug Mueller, Laura and Ken Orabone, Ronit Peskin, Melissa Price, Sunny Savage, David Spahr, Jeremy Umansky, Mia Wasilevich, Butter Wilde, and many others. You're all welcome to dinner at my place anytime (keeping in mind that the accommodations could mean a campsite).

Sam Thayer, thank you for the ongoing gold standard you carry in front of the rest of us forager authors . . . and thank you for the photo. Roey Orbach, thank you so much for the amazing photos. I would be happy just on a professional level, but that I get to call you family is a joyous bonus. Mike Krebill gets a special shout-out for photos, the ongoing support of my work, and the loaned sleeping bags and other gear at wild foods festivals around the United States. Mike, you rock. Danielle Popovitz Salber for helping with some of the photos and a continent-spanning friendship. Ellen Zachos, you know we'll be showing up on each other's doorsteps and toasting with your wild cocktails many, many more times. Here's to decades to come, and thank you for the exquisite photographs.

Ricky Orbach, my love and my best friend: May the adventures continue, and thank you for having my back.

And to Jessy, the best canine foraging companion ever.

GLOSSARY

Alternate: A leaf arrangement in which the leaves attach to the stem from opposite sides not in pairs but singly at different points.

Annual: A plant that completes its entire life cycle—from seed germination to growth, flowering, and producing fruit/seeds—within 1 year or less. Annuals die once they have produced seeds.

Basal: Near ground level; leaves attached at the base of the plant.

Biennial: A plant that spends its first year producing only rosette leaves, then produces a flowering stalk and seeds, after which it dies. Extremely variable, though, because sometimes these plants hang on for a few years before producing seeds. What distinguishes them from perennials is that invariably, once they produce seeds, they die.

Blanch: A quick exposure to boiling water to kill enzymes but usually not long enough to cook the food being blanched.

Blickey: A collection container that straps to one's waist, leaving both hands free.

Bloom: A whitish coating on the surface of a fruit that can be rubbed off. Grapes and plums are examples of fruits that have bloom.

Bract: A modified leaf beneath, and sometimes cupping, a flower or fruit.

Bulb: An underground starch storage organ, such as an onion, in which a tight cluster of overlapping leaves are swollen with stored energy.

Cambium: Just under the dry outer bark, a layer of meristematic cells between the xylem and phloem.

Chaff: The inedible, straw-like parts surrounding the seed or grain that are removed by winnowing.

Deciduous: Plants, especially trees, that drop their leaves at the end of the growing season each year.

Inner bark: The soft layers in between the dry outer bark and the hard wood.

Involucre: The bracts below, and sometimes surrounding, an inflorescence.

Margin: The edge of a leaf.

Meristematic: Plant tissue where cell division and active growth occur; the most tender and choice parts of shoots, rhizomes, and other plant parts from the eater's point of view.

Midrib: The central vein of a leaf.

Mucilaginous: Plant that produces sticky, slimy substances.

Node: The point where leaves join the stem.

Opposite: A leaf arrangement in which the leaves attach to the stem from opposite sides but at the same point, in pairs.

Perennial: A plant that lives for 2 years or more and does not die after producing seeds (unlike biennials).

Phloem: The tissue in plants that moves the sugars created by photosynthesis from the leaves down to the other parts of the plant.

Rhizome: A horizontal underground—or on the surface of the ground—stem.

Root: A plant part that anchors the plant to the earth and also transports water and minerals to the rest of the plant.

Samara: A dry, winged fruit; maple "keys" are samaras.

Sapwood: The soft, recently formed outer layers of a tree's wood between the heartwood and the bark.

Shoot: Vertically and quickly growing stalk of a plant, often directly from the perennial roots. Leaves, if present, are minimal.

Taproot: A single, central root that grows straight down; usually broader toward the soil surface than at the buried growth tip.

Toothed margin: The serrated, jagged edges of a leaf.

Tuber: An underground, modified stem that stores starch. Potatoes are an example of a tuber.

Umbel: A flower cluster with numerous florets arranged on stalks that radiate from the stalk.

Venation: The pattern of veins in a leaf.

Whorl: A leaf arrangement in which the leaves attach to points on the stem in a circle.

Winnow: An action separating edible seeds and grains from the inedible papery parts surrounding them.

Xylem: The water- and mineral-transporting tissues of a plant.

USEFUL RESOURCES

BOOKS

Backyard Foraging: 65 Familiar Plants You Didn't Know You Could Eat by Ellen Zachos. North Adams, MA: Storey Publishing, 2013.

Edible Wild Plants: Wild Foods from Dirt to Plate by John Kallas. Layton, UT: Gibbs Smith, 2010.

The Forager's Feast: How to Identify, Gather, and Prepare Wild Edibles by Leda Meredith. Woodstock, VT: Countryman Press, 2016.

The Forager's Harvest: A Guide to Identifying, Harvesting, and Preparing Edible Wild Plants by Sam Thayer. Bruce, WI: Forager's Harvest Press, 2006.

Hunt, Gather, Cook: Finding the Forgotten Feast by Hank Shaw. Emmaus, PA: Rodale, 2012.

Identifying and Harvesting Edible and Medicinal Plants in Wild (and Not So Wild) Places by Steve Brill. New York: William Morrow Paperbacks, 1994.

Incredible Edibles: 36 Plants That Can Change Your Life by Sam Thayer. Bruce, WI: Forager's Harvest Press, 2017.

The Joy of Foraging by Gary Lincoff. Crestline, Ohio: Crestline Books, 2017.

Making Wild Wines and Meads: 125 Unusual Recipes Using Herbs, Fruits, Flowers & More by Richard Gulling and Pattie Vargas. Revised Edition. North Adams, MA: Storey Publishing, 1999.

National Audubon Society Field Guide to North American Mushrooms. New York: Knopf, 1981.

Nature's Garden: A Guide to Identifying, Harvesting, and Preparing Edible Wild Plants by Sam Thayer. Bruce, WI: Forager's Harvest Press, 2010.

The New Wildcrafted Cuisine: Exploring the Exotic Gastronomy of Local Terroir by Pascal Baudar. White River Junction, VT: Chelsea Green Publishing, 2016.

Northeast Foraging: 120 Wild and Flavorful Edibles from Beach Plums to Wineberries by Leda Meredith. Portland, OR: Timber Press, 2014.

Preserving Everything: Can, Culture, Pickle, Freeze, Ferment, Dehydrate, Salt, Smoke,
  and Store Fruits, Vegetables, Meat, Milk, and More by Leda Meredith. Woodstock,
  VT: Countryman Press, 2014.

Preserving Food without Freezing or Canning: Traditional Techniques Using Salt,
  Oil, Sugar, Alcohol, Vinegar, Drying, Cold Storage, and Lactic Fermentation by the
  Gardeners and Farmers of Terre Vivant. New Edition. White River Junction, VT:
  Chelsea Green Publishing, 2009.

The Scout's Guide to Wild Edibles: Learn How to Forage, Prepare & Eat 40 Wild Foods
  by Mike Krebill. Pittsburgh, PA: St. Lynn's Press, 2016.

Ugly Little Greens: Gourmet Dishes Crafted from Foraged Ingredients by Mia Wasilevich. Boston, MA: Page Street Publishing, 2017.

Wild Fermentation: The Flavor, Nutrition, and Craft of Live Culture Foods by Sandor Ellix
  Katz. Second Edition. White River Junction, VT: Chelsea Green Publishing, 2016.

The Wildcrafted Cocktail: Make Your Own Foraged Syrups, Bitters, Infusions, and Gar-
  nishes by Ellen Zachos. North Adams, MA: Storey Publishing, 2017.

WEBSITES

Foraging Author Websites

www.backyardforager.com (Ellen Zachos)

www.foragersharvest.com (Sam Thayer)

http://garylincoff.com (Gary Lincoff)

https://honest-food.net (Hank Shaw)

www.ledameredith.com (Leda Meredith)

www.transitionalgastronomy.com (Mia Wasilevich)

http://urbanoutdoorskills.com (Pascal Baudar)

www.wildfermentation.com (Sandor Ellix Katz)

http://wildfoodadventures.com (John Kallas)

www.wildmanstevebrill.com (Steve Brill)

Mushroom Expert
www.mushroomexpert.com

National Center for Home Food Preservation
http://nchfp.uga.edu

Virginia Tech Food Preservation
https://ext.vt.edu/food-health/home-food-preservation.html

SOCIAL MEDIA

Instagram

@wildfoodlove, @ledameredith, @foodhistory, @ellenzachos, @lisa.m.rose,
@foragerman, @garylincoff, @tmgastronaut, @pascalbaudar,
@transitionalgastronomy
#foraged, #foraging, #wildfood, #wildfoods, #wildfoodlove

Facebook Groups

Ancestral Plants | Edible Wild Plants | Foragers Unite! | Plant Identification
The Mushroom Identification Forum | Worldwide Wildcrafters

SMARTPHONE APP

Wild Edibles Forage | www.wildmanstevebrill.com/mobile-app.html

RESOURCES FOR BUYING GEAR

Acid Titration Kit, http://grapestompers.com

Blueberry Rake, www.hubbardrakes.com

Davebuilt Nutcracker/Processor, www.davebilt.com

Kenkel Hardshell Nutcracker, www.kenkelnutcracker.com

Nut Wizard, www.nutwizard.com

pH Meter, https://inspectusa.com

Sap Tapping Equipment, www.bascommaple.com

Plus a big shout-out to Sam and Melissa at The Forager's Harvest, who carry a range of
foraging knives, tapping equipment, nutcrackers, foraging books, dehydrators, and more:
www.foragersharvest.com.

INDEX

ABOUT THE AUTHOR

Leda Meredith is a lifelong forager (it's her great-grandmother's fault). She is the author of five previous books including *Northeast Foraging: 120 Wild Edibles from Beach Plums to Wineberries*; *Preserving Everything: Can, Culture, Pickle, Freeze, Ferment, Dehydrate, Salt, Smoke, and Store Fruits, Vegetables, Meat, Milk, and More*; and *The Forager's Feast: How to Identify, Gather, and Prepare Wild Edibles*.

Leda has a certification in Ethnobotany from the New York Botanical Garden where she has been an instructor since 2002. She also teaches for the Brooklyn Botanic Garden and numerous other organizations. She is currently a nomad, traveling around the world with her husband and teaching, foraging, cooking, and botanizing wherever she goes.

You can find out more about her work, contact her, and try some of her delicious wild food recipes via her website www.ledameredith.com.